Charting a Course to

STANDARDS-BASED
GRADING

Charting a Course to

STANDARDS-BASED
GRADING

What to *Stop*, What to *Start*,
and *Why It Matters*

TIM R. WESTERBERG

ASCD
Alexandria, Virginia USA

1703 N. Beauregard St. • Alexandria, VA 22311-1714 USA
Phone: 800-933-2723 or 703-578-9600 • Fax: 703-575-5400
Website: www.ascd.org • E-mail: member@ascd.org
Author guidelines: www.ascd.org/write

Deborah S. Delisle, *Executive Director;* Robert D. Clouse, *Managing Director, Digital Content & Publications;* Stefani Roth, *Publisher;* Genny Ostertag, *Director, Content Acquisitions;* Julie Houtz, *Director, Book Editing & Production;* Miriam Calderone, *Editor;* Thomas Lytle, *Senior Graphic Designer;* Mike Kalyan, *Manager, Production Services;* Circle Graphics, *Typesetter*

PAPERBACK ISBN: 978-1-4166-2263-5   ASCD product #117010 n8/16
PDF E-BOOK ISBN: 978-1-4166-2265-9; see Books in Print for other formats.
Quantity discounts: 10–49, 10%; 50+, 15%; 1,000+, special discounts (e-mail programteam@ascd.org or call 800-933-2723, ext. 5773, or 703-575-5773). For desk copies, go to www.ascd.org/deskcopy.

Library of Congress Cataloging-in-Publication Data

Names: Westerberg, Tim, author.
Title: Charting a course to standards-based grading : what to stop, what to start, and why it matters / Tim R. Westerberg.
Description: Alexandria, VA : ASCD, 2016. | Includes bibliographical references and index.
Identifiers: LCCN 2016022446 (print) | LCCN 2016033223 (ebook) | ISBN 9781416622635 (pbk.) | ISBN 9781416622659 (ebook) | ISBN 9781416622659 (PDF)
Subjects: LCSH: Grading and marking (Students)—Standards.
Classification: LCC LB3051 .W4883 2016 (print) | LCC LB3051 (ebook) | DDC 371.27/2—dc23
LC record available at https://lccn.loc.gov/2016022446

23 22 21 20 19 18 17   2 3 4 5 6 7 8 9 10 11 12

....

This book is dedicated to our family's next generation
of storytellers and writers:
Sadie, Talley, Abbey, and Drue

....

Charting a Course to
STANDARDS-BASED
GRADING

Acknowledgments

Several people and organizations have contributed to my ever-growing understanding of best practices in classroom assessment and grading.

The leading work of Robert Marzano on this topic serves as the research and theoretical foundation for the concepts and recommendations in this book. Dr. Marzano's 2006 book *Classroom Assessment and Grading That Work* and the corresponding training I received from him and others on the ASCD faculty have significantly shaped my thinking on the subject of assessment and grading.

Dr. Karen Spencer-May and the dedicated teachers and administrators of the Omaha Public Schools provided me with one of my first opportunities to field-test the ideas and structures offered here. What I learned from Dr. Spencer-May and her colleagues and the pioneering working documents they developed helped form my classroom assessment and grading theory of action early on in my work on the topic.

Finally, I continue to learn from my long-standing collaborative relationship with Laurie Katagiri-Hoshino and her colleagues at James Campbell High School in Ewa Beach, Hawaii. JCHS began the journey to standards-based grading in 2008 and continues to revise and refine that work to this day. Ms. Katagiri-Hoshino's patience and persistence in bringing classroom assessment and grading best practices to the students at JCHS have kept the standards-based grading vision alive through the ups and downs of this second-order change initiative.

Introduction

What is wrong with this picture?

> The State Board of Education (NC) voted in October to begin the
> 10-point grading scale—in which scores between 90 and 100 earn
> an A—with the 2015–16 school year's freshman class. . . . But the
> State Board will discuss Wednesday whether to start it this fall for
> all high school students. Critics argued it was unfair to keep exist-
> ing students on the seven-point scale—in which scores between 93
> and 100 earn an A. (*The Charlotte Observer,* January 4, 2015)

This is a conversation that is not worth having. Ninety percent, or
93 percent, of what? A 90 in Mr. Martinez's class could, indeed, represent
a much greater knowledge of important course or grade-level content and
skills than a 93 percent in Ms. Lane's class, where students are awarded
extra points for punctuality, turning homework in on time, and bringing in a can of green beans for the Rotary food drive. To get even a 90 in
Mr. Martinez's class might require frequent demonstration of higher-
order cognitive skills as well as content knowledge, whereas in Ms. Lane's
class, half or more of the students receive *As* for scoring 93 or above on
tests that ask for nothing more than short-term recall of basic facts, plus
responsible behavior and a can of green beans.

The discussion in North Carolina could have happened at any level
in almost any state, school district, or school in the United States, and

it reveals a low level of understanding and knowledge about assessment and grading, even among professional educators. This lack of agreement about what grades should be based upon and what grades mean is not a recent phenomenon. Paul Dressel (1957) once provided educators with the following definition of a grade:

> A grade can be regarded only as an inadequate report of an inaccurate judgment by a biased and variable judge of the extent to which a student has attained an undefined level of mastery of an unknown proportion of an indefinite amount of material. (p. 6)

That tongue-in-cheek definition was put forward nearly 60 years ago, a time span longer than the career of almost any educator reading this book. Surely we have come a long way since 1957 in attaining agreement and some level of consistency regarding the purposes and practices of classroom assessment and grading, right? Not really, argues Doug Reeves:

> Neither the weight of scholarship nor common sense seems to have influenced grading policies in many schools. Practices vary greatly among teachers in the same school—and even worse, the practices best supported by research are rarely in evidence. (2008a, p. 85)

Deep and prolonged discussions about classroom assessment and grading practices in general, and about standards-based grading practices in particular, are in order in states, school districts, and schools across the United States. A lot of literature on standards-based grading is already available, much of it quite good. So why this book? Two reasons.

First, my perspective in writing *Charting a Course to Standards-Based Grading: What to Stop, What to Start, and Why It Matters* is shaped by both 30 years as a practitioner in schools and more than a decade working with schools and school districts exploring and implementing effective practices for classroom assessment and grading. As such, my aim is to provide the reader with a concrete, detailed, and practical blueprint for transitioning toward standards-based grading. This book reflects my direct experience with both the thrill of victory and the agony of defeat.

Second, the approach to best practices in assessment and grading put forth in this book allows a school or district to choose which destination or destinations along a progressive continuum of options it wants to move toward, and at what pace.

An analogy drawn from my experience outside education is relevant. I am a member of my local town council, which was recently presented with a proposal to repair and enhance a 25-year-old community amphitheater. The proposal begins with a big-picture look at what might be possible over a period of a decade or more, but then breaks the project down into three distinct phases. The town has the option of choosing to pursue Phase 1, Phases 1 and 2, or all three phases, depending on a variety of factors such as available human and financial resources, fit with the town's overall master plan, and changing community preferences. Changes made during Phase 1 prepare the town to move to Phase 2 if it decides to do so but can also stand alone as significant advancements should local circumstances dictate a halt to further development along the continuum of options.

Schools and districts have unique characteristics and circumstances that determine when it is wise to move ahead with an improvement initiative, and at what pace. Political climate, community receptivity, availability of human and financial resources, topic-specific leadership capacity of teachers and administrators, the presence of a teachable moment (a controversy erupted in the community last spring over how two students vying for valedictorian were graded), and other factors affect the readiness of a school or a district to move to one point or another on the continuum of classroom assessment and grading. This book recognizes that reality and is organized accordingly.

Destination 1, the first stop on the continuum, is for schools or districts that are just beginning to have the conversation about classroom assessment and grading and for the time being just want to "tighten up" a fairly traditional grading system. Six commonly employed practices and one widely shared belief about assessment and grading are exposed for what they are—counterproductive. Schools and districts that chart a course to move from an "everybody do their own thing" approach to common expectations based on best practice will significantly increase the accuracy and fairness of student grades and will have taken a significant step toward developing a system that encourages effort and rewards continued learning. Although probably best conducted districtwide, advancements toward Destination 1 can be made at the school or even individual classroom level.

For some districts the target is to move beyond the limitations of traditional assessment and grading practices to an adopted package of beliefs and practices that actually drive changes in classroom instruction. Earl (2003) reminds us that significant changes in classroom assessment and grading practices have the potential to change virtually every aspect of teaching and learning in schools if we have the vision to use them to do so:

> Changing classroom assessment is the beginning of a revolution—a revolution in classroom practices of all kinds. . . . Getting classroom assessment right is not a simplistic, either-or situation. It is a complex mix of challenging personal beliefs, rethinking instruction, and learning new ways to assess for different purposes. (pp. 15–16)

Destination 2 wraps changes in classroom assessment and grading into the broader context of a district-adopted guaranteed and viable curriculum. Stated simply, a district with a well-developed guaranteed and viable curriculum has identified a limited number of nonnegotiable topics and corresponding leveled performance expectations for every grading period of every grade-level subject (e.g., 5th grade science) and course (e.g., 10th grade biology). Classroom assessments and grades are then built on this structure.

Districts choosing to move toward Destination 2 will need to either first make a stop at Destination 1 or incorporate a discussion of effective and counterproductive assessment and grading practices into their Destination 2 plans. Charting a course to Destination 2 and beyond includes ensuring the presence of organizational conditions necessary to sustain significant change, understanding and executing the steps necessary to create a guaranteed and viable curriculum, and developing a clear vision of what success looks like.

Because Destination 2 involves curricular commitments that extend beyond the influence of individual teachers and schools, this destination and those that follow must be undertaken districtwide. All destinations on our continuum of options for assessment and grading systems call for effective leadership and support; but because Destination 2 requires rethinking, repackaging, and redeveloping curriculum, instruction, and assessment rather than merely tuning up existing practices, a commitment must be made by both administrators and teacher leaders to provide specific supports to those charged with development and implementation. Chapter 11 details those supports.

Destination 3 takes change visibly and directly to the parent community by reporting student achievement by standard rather than, or in addition to, traditional letter grades. At this destination, grade books and report cards look very different from those that students and parents grew up with. As such, community engagement and effective communication—important at every destination—become crucial. Likewise, developing a multiyear plan for moving from a district's starting point through Destinations 1 and 2 and on to Destination 3 becomes absolutely essential. Chapters in the Destination 3 section of this book explore what an implementation plan might include and offer tips on engaging key stakeholder groups in understanding and supporting the central components of a grading and reporting system that is standards based and grounded in a guaranteed and viable curriculum.

Destination 4, competency-based education, is described in Chapter 15. In short, with competency-based education, students advance by demonstrating competency on individual standards or related clusters of standards rather than by passing courses. Course grades are no longer relevant. This is the last stop on the continuum of effective assessment and grading, and it requires a total rethinking of the purposes, nature, and structure of schooling. Competency-based education, a small but growing movement, offers a way to truly individualize education for students.

A clarification is in order here regarding the use in this book of the terms "standards-based grading" and "standards-based education." Here the terms are used to refer to any system of classroom assessment and grading that corresponds to the specifications of Destinations 2 through 4 as described in this book. My argument is that any assessment and grading system bearing a close resemblance to Destinations 2 through 4 must have state or national standards as its starting point—thus making it standards-based.

As referred to in this book, standards-based grading is one component of standards-based education, along with descriptive scoring scales, frequent formative assessment, opportunities for reassessment, trend scoring, the separation of academic achievement and work habits, and valid and reliable assessment tasks, among other research-based, high-probability strategies and practices. Obviously the two terms—"standards-based grading" and "standards-based education"—are given more technical definitions by some researchers and are used somewhat differently by different writers.

This book can be used by individual teachers or teams of teachers to improve day-to-day classroom assessment and grading practices, which is the essence of Destination 1. But the intended primary audiences are school and district leadership teams—teams of teachers and administrators charged with leading and supporting a journey to systemic change. *Charting a Course to Standards-Based Grading* serves as a guidebook for that journey.

DESTINATION 1

Addressing Seven Counterproductive Assessment and Grading Practices and Beliefs

· · · · · · · · · · · · ·

Classroom assessment and grading practices in the United States are buttressed by fervently held, time-honored practices and beliefs. Furthermore, they are autonomous in the sense that, in many schools and districts, at least, they are left to the judgment of individual teachers, outside the purview of colleagues and supervisors save a few generalities such as treating everyone the same.

And it is not just teachers who regard selecting assessment and grading practices as individual professional prerogatives. For the most part, students and parents accept this ingrained enfranchisement. What the teacher says goes, provided she shows no favoritism, can provide numerical data supporting a grade, and is at least somewhat within the bounds of what adults experienced when they were in school. In many school districts, board policies and negotiated contracts support the accepted norm of the teacher as the sole determiner of student grades, arrived at by whatever method and means she deems appropriate.

Teachers—not administrators, students, or parents—*should* be the final determiners of student grades. After all, teachers observe and evaluate their students' academic performance every day for an entire grading period. No one else has gathered as much data upon which to base a conclusion about student mastery of identified content and skills as has a student's teacher.

Likewise, classroom assessment and grading should be grounded in practices and beliefs that are transparent, shared, and supported by research. And therein lies the problem—in too many U.S. classrooms, grades are determined by practices that are ill defined, unique to individual teachers, and counterproductive. In too many U.S. schools, it can be said that a student's grade depends, to a significant degree, upon which teacher the computer assigns that student to.

Destination 1 exposes seven counterproductive assessment and grading practices and beliefs prevalent—and in some cases accepted without question—in U.S. classrooms and schools. Improving accuracy, fairness, and student learning while maintaining many traditional grading practices is the goal of charting a course to Destination 1.

• • • • • • • • • • • • • •

The Zero

At a conference in San Antonio in 2007, Doug Reeves asked participants to determine the unit or topic grade a student should receive given the data in Figure 1.1, using each of three grading scales. The grades in Figure 1.1 are all on the same topic or skill, all comprehensive, and all of the same weight (all tests, or all labs, or all demonstrations). Note that under Method 1, the method most often used in the United States, the student receives a failing grade in spite of strong performances near the culmination of the unit or grading period. On the other hand, by changing nothing but the intervals between scores (Method 2), the student receives a *C–* for the same level of performance.

It should be obvious that for students in this or similar situations, the scale the teacher uses to calculate a final topic grade makes the difference between passing and failing the topic—and perhaps between graduating or dropping out of school. If your son or daughter were in this class and struggling, would it be OK with you if the computer assigned him or her to a teacher using Method 1 when a teacher of the same course across the hall used Method 2—and if the principal defended the process in the name of academic freedom for teachers?

Using your teacher judgment (Method 3), what final topic grade would you give this student, unencumbered by a district-mandated grading scale, if the criterion were assigning a grade that best reflects the student's

FIGURE 1.1

Topic Grades as Determined by Various Grading Methods

Grades in Chronological Order	Method 1 70 (*D*), 80 (*C*), 90 (*B*), 100 (*A*)	Method 2 0 (*F*), 1 (*D*), 2 (*C*), 3 (*B*), 4 (*A*)	Method 3 Teacher Judgment
C	80	2	
C	80	2	
MA	0	0	
D	70	1	
C	80	2	
B	90	3	
MA	0	0	
MA	0	0	
B	90	3	
A	100	4	
Topic Grade	59% (*F*)	1.7 (*C*–)	?

MA = missing assignment

Source: Used with permission. Adapted from *Elements of Grading: A Guide to Effective Practice (2nd ed.)* by Douglas Reeves. Copyright 2016 by Solution Tree Press, 555 North Morton Street, Bloomington, IN 47404, 800.733.6786, SolutionTree.com. All rights reserved.

demonstrated mastery of topic content and skills at the end of instruction? Posing this question to thousands of teachers and administrators at workshops and conferences over the last decade consistently yields results of more than half of each group indicating a grade of *A* or *B* based on the student's growth and performance at the conclusion of instruction.

Depending on the scale and method of grading chosen by individual teachers, a student could earn anything from an *A* to an *F* for the same academic performance. So much for the accuracy, objectivity, and fairness of traditional grading practices.

Why do we insist on using an assessment and grading system that yields results that fly in the face of teacher judgment?

It is common practice in U.S. schools for teachers to enter zeros into the grade book for missing assignments. The effects of this practice on students' grades vary considerably depending on the type of grading scale used, but the most counterproductive effects accompany the most commonly used scale—the 100-point or percentage scale.

The Zero's Deadly Effects

In addition to the problems associated with mixing academic performance with work ethic (a topic covered in Chapter 3), there are at least three reasons why using zeros for missing work on the 100-point scale is counterproductive.

The first reason is mathematical. For example, with a grading scale that uses intervals of 60–69, 70–79, 80–89, and 90–100, there is a 60-point gap between a zero and a *D,* whereas a gap of only 10 points separates a *D* and a *C,* a *C* and a *B,* and a *B* and an *A.* The effect of that difference in range is to give missing assignments considerably more weight in determining a final grade than assignments of the same type (test for test, homework for homework, paper for paper, etc.) that were completed. Expressed another way, after receiving a zero it takes a whole lot of 100s to get the cumulative grade up to a *D*–.

A teacher using this approach might be advised to announce to students and parents at the beginning of each term that, although the course is titled Algebra 1, for example, the grading methods employed expose the fact that it is really a work-ethic course—missing work counts for much more than work turned in demonstrating mastery of course content and skills. "We do a little algebra in here, but this course is mostly about work ethic."

The second reason why entering zeros for missing work on the 100-point scale is counterproductive has to do with the effect of that practice on student motivation. As just noted, it can be very difficult to recover, gradewise, from a single zero, let alone multiple zeros. The result is that students facing such a situation often give up, having figured out that even if they work hard for the remainder of the term they will still end up failing the class. The math is against them. The result is disengagement and absenteeism at best, behavior problems and dropping out of school at worst.

Teachers sometimes communicate the hopelessness of the situation directly to students. High school counselors have experienced situations in which a student comes to the office, often fairly early in the grading period, asking to be dropped from a class, stating, "The teacher says there is no way I can pass the class, so I might as well drop out." Such a request is a sad statement and counterproductive to our goals as educators.

Finally, including zeros in the calculation reduces the validity of grades and misrepresents actual student proficiency, thereby eroding the accuracy of grades as indicators of knowledge of subject or course content and skills proficiency. It is unlikely that a student knows absolutely nothing—zero—about the content or skills under study. In fact, good teachers believe that it would be impossible given their expert instruction for a student who attends class even part-time to learn absolutely nothing—"I'm too good for that." A zero for missing work undermines the validity of any cumulative grade of which it is a part in that it measures something other than mastery of course content and skills.

Alternatives to the Zero

So, what alternatives are available for dealing with missing assignments besides recording and counting zeros in a 100-point, percentage system?

The percentage system usually entails lumping all points earned during a grading period together and dividing by the total points possible to arrive at a term-average percentage that is then converted to a letter grade. Arithmetic averages or mean scores are disproportionately affected by extreme scores, and a zero in a 100-point system is an extreme score because of the disproportionate range between it and the lowest passing grade, as discussed earlier.

One alternative is to calculate the median and mode scores for a unit of instruction, perhaps in addition to the mean score, to see which measure of central tendency best represents students' demonstrated knowledge of identified subject or course content and skills. Median and mode scores are not as sensitive to extreme scores as is the mean.

A second option is to assign a range-equivalent score to missing work instead of a zero. For example, in the *D*-to-*A* scale of 60 to 100 points, a score of 50 could be entered into the grade book for missing assignments, which has the effect of weighting missing assignments the same as completed assignments of the same type. This approach addresses the mathematical issue associated with zeros in the 100-point system—unequal intervals between grades. The problem with this approach, and the reason I do not recommend it, is that it does not play well politically. Districts that have floated this approach to missing work (for example, Dallas and Nashville) have often faced a backlash from teachers, parents, and board members. "What? Students are given 50 percent for doing nothing?" Although the approach is mathematically justifiable, awarding students points for work not done, even if the point value recorded is below failing, just doesn't feel right.

A third option is to jettison the 100-point scale in favor of a scale with equal intervals. For example, instead of the percentage system, assessment tasks could be scored on a 0-to-4 scale tied to a corresponding descriptive scoring scale, with uniform intervals between scores and zeros used for missing work. This is the scale I recommend and a topic explored in detail in Destination 2. Figure 1.2 shows how an urban district in the Midwest transitioned from a 100-point scale to an equal-interval scale, in this case with points ranging from 0 to 12. Note that students still receive zeros for missing work—there is no free lunch here. The difference between this scale and the 100-point scale is that of equal intervals.

Now look at the difference this change makes when calculating unit or topic final grades for four hypothetical students, as depicted in Figure 1.3. The grades reported in the second column of Figure 1.3 are for

FIGURE 1.2

Moving From a 100-Point to an Equal-Interval Scale

100–98	A+	12
97–95	A	11
94–93	A–	10
92–90	B+	9
89–86	B	8
85–84	B–	7
83–81	C+	6
80–77	C	5
76–75	C–	4
74–73	D+	3
72–71	D	2
70	D–	1
≤69	F	0

different assessments of the same standard or topic, not different topics, and are listed in chronological order, left to right. Zeros indicate missing assignments.

We do not know why the first student demonstrated a high level of mastery of the targeted measurement topic three consecutive times and then failed to complete the last assessment—and that information is important. What we do know is that almost all teachers viewing these data do not feel, at the gut level, that a grade of *D+* best reflects that student's knowledge of the targeted material. And even fewer teachers say they would fail the second and fourth students.

FIGURE 1.3
Grading Scale Comparisons

	Grades	Cumulative Grade Based on 100-Point Grading Scale	Cumulative Grade Based on 0- to 12-Point Grading Scale
Student 1	A+, A+, A+, 0	D+ (75)	B+ (9)
Student 2	C, 0, C, C	F (60)	C− (3.75)
Student 3	C, A−, 0, B, B, C	D (72)	C+ (6)
Student 4	D, D, D, D, 0, D, D	F (62)	D (1.7)

Again, one wonders, *Why do we insist on using an assessment and grading system that yields results that fly in the face of teacher judgment?*

A strong argument asserts that failing to complete assigned work is a behavioral problem that should be dealt with using behavioral rather than academic consequences. Therefore, a fourth option for dealing with missing assignments is to insist that they be completed using natural consequences such as student contracts, parent involvement and sanctions, lunch detention, and Saturday school as leverage.

For too many students, getting a zero for missing work and moving on is a reward—"Thank you. I didn't want to do the work in the first place." The natural consequence for not doing your work is having to do it—at a time and place not necessarily of your liking.

The Zeros Aren't Permitted (ZAP) program is designed to increase expectations for students who repeatedly or occasionally fail to complete and turn in homework assignments or projects on time. ZAP emphasizes the belief that homework assignments and projects are important and must be completed. A number of school websites, including those of Norco Intermediate (http://www.cnusd.k12.ca.us/domain/4511), Costa Mesa High School/Middle School (http://cmhs.nmusd.us/zap), Guyer High School (http://www.dentonisd.org/site/Default.aspx?PageID=6468), and Jemez Mountain Public Schools (http://www.jmsk12.com/?page_id=1743), list ZAP strategies that teachers and schools use to enforce the expectation that choosing not to do assignments is not an option—or at least not an option without consequences.

A final alternative to averaging in zeros for missing work is trend scoring, which is now included as an option in most grading software. The central concept is to assign a final topic grade or score based on a student's growth over the course of instruction rather than averaging scores earned at the beginning of instruction with scores earned later on. The assumption is that, with effective instruction, students will experience growth over time. Of course, some students may decide to disengage and therefore will receive lower scores later in a unit of instruction, but such disengagement suggests an emotional/behavioral problem that should be dealt with using emotional/behavioral strategies. With trend scoring, data points for missing assignments may not be significant factors when assigning final topic grades or scores if enough other evidence exists to support a conclusion. Chapter 4 includes more discussion of trend scoring.

Other solutions to the zero problem are offered in literature on the topic (see, for example, Guskey, 2004; O'Connor, 2009a; Reeves, 2004; and Wormeli, 2006). Of course, every solution presents its own drawbacks. The point isn't that there is one right approach to the problem of missing work, but rather that it is wrong to simply ignore this elephant in the room.

• • • • • • • • • • • • • • •

We have an obligation to our students and to our communities to collectively study the zero issue and its possible solutions, to define a shared approach to dealing with the problem, and to communicate that approach and its supporting beliefs and values to all stakeholders. Simply making people aware of the inordinate power of the zero—and the unintended consequences—can be an eye-opener and a good first step.

Extra Credit

Extra credit is, by definition, extra. Whatever it consists of lies outside identified grade-level or course standards. If tasks associated with extra credit were directly tied to grade-level or course standards, they would not be "extra."

Including performances on tasks that assess content or skills not assigned to the associated grade level or course in topic, grade-level, or course grades negatively affects the validity of those grades. Neatly coloring in a poster is not a valid measure of reading comprehension. Therefore, extra credit has no place in a valid system of classroom assessment and grading. The situation actually becomes humorous if we are talking about standards-based grading: standards-based grades not based on course standards?

From Bringing in Green Beans to Watching a Play: The Many Forms of Extra Credit

Some forms of extra credit are more obvious than others. Somewhere today students are receiving extra credit in mathematics for contributing boxes of tissues to the classroom supply, for cleaning up the chemistry lab, for turning off their cell phones in English, and for bringing a can of green beans to history class in support of the school's food drive. To be sure, there is nothing wrong with schools encouraging students to aid the less fortunate or contribute to the common good, but they should label and report such activity for what it is—"citizenship" or something else along those lines—not mathematics, or history, or science.

Other extra-credit tasks are not as easy to identify. What about credit in an English class for attending a school play? If students are asked to write a literary critique on the play and writing a literary critique is among the course standards, the assignment may not be "extra." However, if a teacher awards credit for simply attending the play because she believes going to a play is a good experience for young adults, it is green beans in a different form.

Retaining Differentiated Instruction and Reassessment

This position against extra credit does not conflict with the call for teachers to differentiate instruction to address unique student needs. Students who quickly demonstrate mastery of topic content and skills at the basic and proficient levels should be given opportunities to work at the advanced level for that grade level on that topic or standard. Such opportunities do not fall into the category of extra credit as long as the work students are asked to do is tied to the topic or standard under study. Students who are given opportunities to learn content or demonstrate skills in a way different from that presented to the whole class are not doing extra credit as long as what they are doing advances them toward mastery of one or more of the standards addressed in the unit of study.

Nor should the prohibition against extra credit be misinterpreted as opposition to providing students with opportunities for reassessment. We should be encouraging students to learn from mistakes on initial assessments and give them opportunities to demonstrate knowledge of essential content and skills at a later time. What is important is that all students learn what is being studied, not that they are all able to demonstrate that learning on the first attempt and at the exact same moment.

If particular content or skills are worth teaching and assessing the first time, they are worth reteaching and reassessing when students are not successful. Saying, "I don't have time to reteach and reassess" suggests that it is OK for some students not to demonstrate understanding of the topic, which raises the question of why the content or skill was selected for study in the first place.

Reteaching and reassessing do, indeed, take time, but students are better served by ensuring that they learn a few really critical concepts and skills well than by exposing them only superficially to many. Technology can help facilitate the reteaching and reassessment processes. For example, the software developer Educreations has apps that allow you to record your voice and capture images from your iPad screen; import documents and pictures from your photo library, Dropbox, or Google Drive; or insert a webpage to create video tutorials that students can access any time.

However, the opportunity to reassess comes with conditions. First, students must bring something to the table to earn the opportunity for a second chance to demonstrate understanding. That is, students must demonstrate that they have done something to learn the content or skills being evaluated. "Show me that you've completed all missing homework assignments for this unit, and then we'll talk about a reassessment." "Complete the computer tutorial on this topic, and then I'll let you give it another shot." "Come in for help during lunch on Tuesday, and we'll see how you do."

Students are given reassessment opportunities because we want them to learn the material, not because we want to give them an incentive to blow off initial assessments in hopes of getting lucky a second time around. Raising grades for students who have learned from earlier mistakes is a valid assessment strategy. Allowing students to "go fishing" is allowing them to game the system.

The second condition for providing reassessment opportunities is that the teacher has the right to set deadline dates, usually coinciding with the end of the unit of study or shortly thereafter. "Students, on Monday we will finish this two-week unit on *The Great Gatsby*. All reassessments must be completed on Wednesday."

One reason setting a deadline may make sense is that, for some content in particular, genuine learning has an expiration date. We have to question the utility of attempting to demonstrate understanding in November of a concept that was part of a unit that began and ended in September.

The second reason it makes sense to set a deadline for reassessment is to make the whole reassessment process manageable for teachers. It is ludicrous to expect teachers to manage anytime, on-demand reassessment opportunities in addition to teaching and assessing the current unit of study.

People frequently raise the concern that offering reassessment opportunities does not prepare students for college and the so-called real world. "Students are not going to get to do assessments over when they get to college, and employers expect their employees to get it right the first time. We're promoting the development of false expectations." The response to this concern has several aspects.

First, the students we are talking about are elementary and secondary students, not college students or full-time adult employees. The differences in age, maturity, and mandatory versus voluntary involvement merit consideration of differences in treatment.

The second aspect, which is related to the first, is the fact that we are preparing students to transition into postsecondary education and work, which invites consideration of a more lenient reassessment policy for younger students and a more restricted policy for high school juniors and seniors.

Third, the real world of college and work is not all that black and white. Some colleges and universities are beginning to offer features of standards-based grading in their classes. For example, classes in some institutions now include online practice quizzes (formative assessment) that students can retake if not successful on their first attempts (reassessment). Graduate students at many colleges and universities are able to run their theses past their committees for suggested improvements (formative assessment) before the final judgment day (summative assessment). Law students can retake the bar exam until they pass (reassessment). These examples are intended to suggest not that such practices are the norm in higher education, but that classroom assessment and grading practices are evolving, even at that level.

Wormeli (2011) points out that the work world often affords adults the opportunity to keep learning until they get it right:

> The teacher who claims to be preparing students for the working world by disallowing all redos forgets that adult professionals actually flourish through redos, retakes, and do-overs. LSAT. MCAT. Praxis. Bar exam. CPA exam. Driver's licensure. Pilot's licensure. Auto mechanic certification exam. Every one of these assessments reflects the adult-level, working-world responsibilities our students will one day face. Many of them are high stakes: People's lives depend on these tests' validity as accurate measures of individual competence. All of them can be redone over and over for full credit.

On a more personal note, had I been held to a standard of "get it right the first time or else" during my 31 years as a teacher and a principal, I would have been unemployed since 1973—my first year of teaching.

Finally, even if standards-based assessment and grading practices are not mirrored at the college and university level in many cases, college admissions officers and professors continue to state that what they want from K–12 education are graduates who can read and understand complex texts, write cogently, think analytically and creatively, and demonstrate a command of discipline-specific foundational content and skills. Standards-based education done right (clear learning goals aligned with college-readiness standards, cognitively demanding performance expectations, and grades based solely on demonstrated mastery of grade-level course content and skills) can deliver such graduates. So although the specific grading practices may change, students will enter college with the knowledge and skills needed to be successful.

I offer one final note on reassessment. The reassessment score should replace the score from the earlier attempt, not be averaged with it. The reason is pretty straightforward—the reassessment score is the most accurate representation of what the student now knows or can do. An average of two or more assessment scores on the same content or skill is not representative of what the student knew or could do at any point in time.

Extra credit, no. Reassessment with conditions, yes.

Combining Academic Performance with Work Ethic and Citizenship

Consider the following descriptions of two students in the same high school chemistry class.

B. J. is an exceptionally bright student. She gets *As* on all summative assessments—labs, quizzes, and tests—but she does not do any homework or other outside-of-class work, receiving zeros on all those assignments. In most U.S. schools, B. J. would get a grade that represents some sort of an average of those two extremes, let's say a *C.* Nevertheless, following high school she goes on to graduate from college after three and a half years with double majors in chemistry and Arabic (B. J. is a native English speaker).

W. T. does not really like chemistry and has no intention of pursuing a science-related course of study after high school. He is a humanities guy and enjoys hanging out backstage in the theater during his free time. He took chemistry because his counselor told him that three years of science "looks good on your transcript." But W. T. is the poster child for strong work ethic and citizenship. He completes every assignment—usually error ridden, but turned in on time. He is never tardy or absent and contributes to class in every way possible, including staying late to clean up after a lab activity. W. T. is so trustworthy that his teacher hires him some weekends as a babysitter. He gets all possible points for homework, class participation, and extra-credit opportunities, but he gets Ds and Fs on summative assessments. In most U.S. schools, W. T. would get some sort of an average of those two extremes, let's say a C.

Those two students are nothing alike—at least as far as chemistry class goes—yet they both leave high school with exactly the same grade on their transcripts. B. J. is brilliant. A major pharmaceutical firm should consider hiring her, as she just might discover a life-changing drug someday. But be forewarned—she might not come to work on time or follow company policy in all respects. As for W. T., hire him. He is trustworthy, loyal, and totally dependable. But do not put him in your pharmacy to dispense drugs—he might accidentally kill somebody!

Combining Apples and Oranges

These two examples illustrate the problem with combining academic performance and work ethic and citizenship into one grade. Once again, it is a validity problem. The students' performance related to chemistry content makes it impossible to draw any conclusions about their work ethic, and their work ethic performance confounds any conclusions regarding competency in chemistry. The single grade—C, in the case of B. J. and W. T.—is rendered all but meaningless.

The obvious solution to this problem is to evaluate, record, and report two separate grades—one based on students' demonstrated mastery of course academic standards and one for work ethic and citizenship. Both grades could be shown on report cards and even transcripts.

If a single course grade is required for official records, school or district policy should clearly spell out how that grade is to be determined. One option is to report both academic and work ethic grades but to use only the academic grade as the official course grade. Another option is to combine both grades according to some predetermined ratio (for example, 95 percent academic, 5 percent work ethic).

If the decision is to base a single course grade on a combination of academic performance and work ethic, the weights given to each category should, at the very least, be consistent across all teachers of the same course. A strong argument can be made for extending that consistency to the department or grade, school, or even district level. With either option—academic grade only or a combination—the values that underlie the decision should reflect input from and be clearly communicated to all stakeholders.

Standards-based purists generally recommend basing the official course grade on academic performance only. They attest that work ethic and citizenship should be taught, evaluated, and reported on report cards or progress reports but not included in course grades.

The reason for this recommendation was mentioned earlier—the problems that result from combining apples and oranges. However, some schools and districts have chosen to transition to standards-based grading by starting with the combination approach in the face of initial teacher, student, and parent perceptions that the real-life importance of hard work and dependability is devalued when only academic performance is considered. Better give a little than risk losing the entire grading initiative because of community pushback, so that argument goes.

One might ask, "What's the point of recording academic and work ethic scores separately if, in the end, the system forces us to come up with one final course grade?" Part of the answer has already been addressed—the recommendation that both academic and work ethic performance be evaluated and reported but that only academic performance be used to determine the grade of record, thus preserving the validity of the course grade as an indicator of mastery of course standards.

The other and most important response to the "What's the point?" question focuses squarely on student learning. When we record progress by attaching assessment results to topic or unit standards, both academic and behavioral, students can more clearly see exactly what their strengths and weaknesses are (see Chapter 12 for more on grade book organization). "I'm doing well in reading comprehension and literary analysis but need to work on persuasive writing and staying on task in class." In contrast, "Your grade in this class at this time is a 78" provides little or no guidance on how to improve.

Communicating What Counts

It is important to communicate, particularly to students and parents, that even when final course grades are based solely on demonstrated academic performance, work ethic and citizenship do "count." With rare exception, students who complete all their work and are engaged during class will perform better on summative assessments than they would have otherwise. If that is not the case for most students—that is, if students seem to perform about the same on summative assessments whether they do the work or not—one has to question the relevance and quality of classroom activities, assignments, and instruction in general.

So when students ask, for example, if homework counts for anything, the correct answer is "Yes, those of you who worked hard on today's assignment will see the results on the test next week." When conducting "post-mortem" reviews following summative assessments, teachers should explicitly point out the link between class activities and assignments and summative assessment results. "Remember last week's homework on combining like terms? There it is on yesterday's test—items 17 through 21. Those of you who did that homework assignment did better on those items, and thus got better grades on this test, than those of you who did not."

What about the student who can do well on summative assessments without doing all the work? That student is not properly challenged and perhaps even misplaced in the class, and the teacher and other school personnel have an obligation to work with him or her to address that situation. As far as the course grade goes, an *A* accurately reflects the student's demonstrated performance on course academic standards, although perhaps not his or her work ethic.

Failure to engage in classroom activities and assignments is a behavioral problem and should thus be dealt with using behavior strategies and consequences. To penalize or reward students academically for behavioral issues is to combine academic and work ethic performances—a violation of best practices in classroom assessment and grading.

Averaging

Averaging is evil! OK, that claim calls for some explanation.

There are certainly times in classroom assessment and grading processes when averaging is called for. When a teacher is required to come up with a single composite score or grade to represent student performance on several related but different standards or measurement topics—for example, a grade for 7th grade science that consists of units on the structure and properties of matter, chemical reactions, and forces and motion—the best indicator of overall course achievement might well be an average of the final scores for each of the three topics.

Also, when assessment scores fail to show normal learning-curve growth over the course of instruction—that is, when scores for an individual student or for a group of students are widely divergent due to a variety of possible and fairly common measurement errors—a measure of central tendency (mean, median, or mode) may represent the best fit for the assessment data.

Measurement error notwithstanding, averaging is evil when used to determine a final score for a single measurement topic. Continuing with the example from 7th grade science, averaging should not be used to determine the final topic score for the unit on chemical reactions, which was assessed multiple times during the course of instruction. Instead, trend scoring, a method that was briefly mentioned in Chapter 1, yields the most accurate representation of what students know about chemical reactions at the end of instruction.

What's Wrong with Averaging?

Before getting into the details of trend scoring, it is important to explore why averaging is not the best method to use when calculating a final score for a specific measurement topic. Averaging assumes that no learning has occurred during the course of instruction. That is, averaging gives the same weight to an in-class assessment administered early in the unit on chemical reactions, when students were on the front end of the learning curve, as it does to a similar assessment given at the end of the unit after students have had the benefit of instruction. Ken O'Connor (2009a) provides the example shown in Figure 4.1.

Using the data in the figure, consider the following two questions: (1) How do you feel about giving all four students the same final topic grade? (2) How do you feel about failing (63 percent is an *F* in many classrooms) all four students on this topic? Note that the data do not represent scores on 10 different topics, but rather 10 composite assessments on the same topic.

We can draw several observations and conclusions from these data. Here are a few.

First, no teacher worth continued employment would allow Alex to continue to receive the same low score on 10 consecutive assessments without intervening in the teaching and learning process. Obviously the approach Alex is taking to learning this topic or the approach the teacher is using to teach this topic—or both—are not working for Alex. So after the second or third score of 63, Alex's teacher should pull him aside to talk about making some changes.

We do not know why Jennifer performed poorly at the beginning of the unit (personal problems, lack of important background knowledge, complacency?), but after the second or third score of 100, Jennifer needs to move on to some more difficult material within the topic. She does not need to complete five more worksheets on balancing equations—she gets it!

FIGURE 4.1
Problems with the Mean

Assessments in Order	Karen	Alex	Jennifer	Stephen
Assessment #1	0	63	0	0
Assessment #2	0	63	10	0
Assessment #3	0	63	10	62
Assessment #4	90	63	10	62
Assessment #5	90	63	100	63
Assessment #6	90	63	100	63
Assessment #7	90	63	100	90
Assessment #8	90	63	100	90
Assessment #9	90	63	100	100
Assessment #10	90	63	100	100
Total	630	630	630	630
Mean	63%	63%	63%	63%
Median	90%	63%	100%	63%
Mode	90%	63%	100%	?

Source: From *How to Grade for Learning, K–12* (p. 155), by Ken O'Connor, 2009, Thousand Oaks, CA: Corwin. Copyright 2009 by Corwin. Reprinted with permission.

Likewise, the teacher will want to help Karen find out what one thing is tripping her up so she can move on to more advanced work with Jennifer.

And then there is Stephen. Stephen knew little or nothing about this topic at the start of instruction. That's why he took the course. But Stephen is a model student. He worked hard, completed every homework assignment, and came in after school and attended National Honor Society tutoring sessions for extra help. Stephen never gave up, and by the end of the unit he was nailing it. And for that you are going to reward Stephen with an *F*? That is what Stephen gets for this unit if we average his scores.

Trend Scoring: The Preferred Alternative

A more accurate final representation of what each student knows and can do with regard to this topic would involve looking at student performance near the end of instruction, or each student's learning trend. In this case, using that approach means that only Alex would fail.

Teachers tend to use trend scoring naturally because it makes "teacher gut" sense; not many would fail all four students in the scenarios just described. What does your teacher gut tell you would be the most accurate final topic score for each of the three students whose individual scores are shown here?

Student 1	Student 2	Student 3
2.0	3.0	2.0
1.5	2.0	1.0
2.0	2.0	1.5
3.0	2.5	2.0
2.5	3.0	2.0
3.0	2.0	2.5
3.0	3.0	3.0
2.5	2.5	3.0
3.0	3.0	3.5
3.0	3.0	3.0

Once again, these data represent 10 assessment scores on the same topic and are in chronological order from top to bottom. Most educators would feel comfortable giving all three students a final topic score of 3.0, although an argument can be made for something higher than that for the third student. But if you average the scores, the results for Students 1, 2, and 3 are 2.55, 2.60, and 2.35, respectively. At the same time, their trend scores are 3.00, 2.71, and 3.00, respectively.

Once again, *Why do we insist on using an assessment and grading system that yields results that fly in the face of teacher judgment?*

Before leaving these data, we can make an observation regarding the practice of including zeros for missing work in the calculation of topic grades, as discussed in Chapter 1. Let's reconsider the three students' scores, but with each of them now having a missing assignment:

Student 1	Student 2	Student 3
2.0	3.0	2.0
1.5	2.0	1.0
2.0	2.0	1.5
3.0	2.5	MA
2.5	3.0	2.0
MA	2.0	2.5
3.0	3.0	3.0
2.5	2.5	3.0
3.0	MA	3.5
3.0	3.0	3.0

MA = missing assignment

With the concept of trend scoring in mind, do we need those data points to arrive at final topic scores? Most educators would answer no. Substitute any value from 1 to 4 for the missing assignments, and the conclusion about competency at the end of instruction remains the same.

This is what happens with software-generated trend scoring—missing assignments are treated as measurement errors (it is unlikely that the students know absolutely nothing about the topic, especially given their other assessment scores) and thus given little weight by the algorithm used to calculate final topic scores. Of course, the missing assignments are important if we are evaluating and recording work ethic or if the school or district has identified behavioral strategies and consequences that are to be deployed to reinforce the importance of personal responsibility.

Previous discussions regarding trend scoring have relied on "eyeballing" the data to arrive at a final topic score. Teachers and administrators are understandably uncomfortable with such an approach to determining grades as it appears to be arbitrary when justifying grades to students and parents. Fortunately, most grading software programs now have a trend-scoring option. The algorithm built into the software is based on a concept called the Power Law of Learning, and its effect is illustrated in Figure 4.2.

The software algorithm calculates the best-fit true score given the assessment data entered, weighting scores entered later in the instructional unit more heavily than scores entered early on. A minimum of three assessment scores is needed to establish a trend, but five or more scores are recommended to increase accuracy.

Doug Reeves (2008a) identifies averaging, along with zeros for missing work and the "semester killer" (the make-or-break test, project, lab, or other assignment, discussed in the next chapter), as a practice so ineffective as to be labeled "toxic." Is it time to send your classroom assessment and grading practices to detox?

FIGURE 4.2
Bar Graph with Power Law Scores

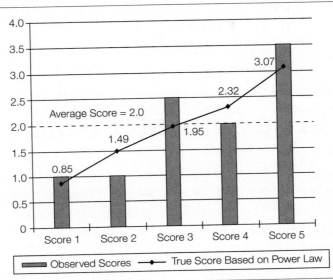

The Semester Killer

At a high school where I served as principal, it was the 10th grade English research paper. It was worth two trillion points, about the same as our national debt, and was equally impossible to dig one's way out of. The semester killer.

OK, two trillion points is hyperbole. What is not an exaggeration is that at that well-respected school and at many others across the United States, students who have produced satisfactory work for the bulk of a semester fail a course because of a single assignment given disproportionate weight (points) vis-à-vis assignments tied to other course standards.

The problems associated with the semester killer are, of course, not restricted to high schools or to the research paper. Fifth grade students in my district once spent several weeks constructing covered wagons, ostensibly as a learning strategy designed to address something related to the grade-level curricular unit on the Westward Expansion. The students loved the project. Student engagement levels were high, as was parent involvement. And of course because the project went on for weeks, it was assigned a number of points that outweighed anything else done that grading period.

The reader has no doubt already identified a number of assessment and grading issues stemming from this scenario. The project was not directly tied to any grade-level standard or cluster of related standards, thus disqualifying it, by definition, as a standards-based assignment. Even if grade-level standards had been identified that would justify the project, there was no discussion as to whether building covered wagons was *the best* strategy to reach those standards. Contextual factors, including student background knowledge, expectations regarding cognitive rigor, formative and summative assessment design, other instructional strategies employed, and time limitations, must be taken into consideration when selecting instructional strategies.

And of course, pertinent to the topic of this chapter, the question of whether the weight given the project in relationship to the overall importance of all grade-level standards and assignments for that grading period remained unexamined in my district. How many 5th graders over the years received lowered or even failing grades because they weren't artistic or because their parents didn't have the time to do the project for them?

What other semester killers are out there waiting to strike? Science fair projects? Group presentations? Book reports? Exhibitions? This is not to say that projects, reports, presentations, exhibitions, and the like are in and of themselves inappropriate or inconsistent with classroom assessment and grading best practices. To the contrary, such tasks often offer the best opportunity for students to practice and demonstrate higher-order thinking skills. Rather the point is that such tasks must be standards-based and evaluated vis-à-vis the potential effectiveness and time commitments associated with other high-probability instructional strategies.

Take a moment to reflect on the major assignments given to students in your classroom or in the classrooms of those you coach or supervise and the weights assigned to those assignments in determining course grades. Are they justified given the criteria discussed above?

Who Suffers the Most

It is the student in the middle, the *C–* student, who is most often the victim of the knockout punch delivered by a heavily weighted, long-term project such as a research paper. High-performing students do everything asked of them in their quest to amass as many total points as possible, so of course they will complete the assignment. Low-performing students are prone to give up on this assignment, as they have on many other class assignments, without even giving it a try. Meanwhile, the student in the midrange of the grade distribution completes some aspects of the project but lacks the planning and organizational skills and the self-confidence and "grit" needed to see it through to the end. His or her overall 78 percent in the course drops to a 56 percent, and thus a student who has demonstrated at least a basic level of proficiency on four of five course standards fails the entire semester.

It should be noted that in a true standards-based school, a school in which students advance standard by standard, a student in this situation would need to continue working on the research standard but not the others. However, in most schools it is all or nothing—a compensatory approach to grading in which the challenge is to collect enough overall points during the grading period to earn a passing grade regardless of performance on individual course or grade-level standards. Demonstrate proficiency on three of five standards with an overall 70 percent, and you are given a grade that suggests proficiency on all course standards. Demonstrate proficiency on four out of five course standards with an overall 69 percent, and you receive a grade that suggests a lack of proficiency on all course standards.

Common Missteps

When asked why the semester killer is assigned so much weight in determining a final course grade, teachers often reference the amount of class time devoted to the assignment. However, in a standards-based system, it is the importance of the standard itself, rather than the time spent on a single assignment, that should be considered in arriving at an overall course or subject grade. If the research standard is twice as essential to future academic success as all other course standards combined, then that standard should be given a corresponding weight in calculating an overall course grade, regardless of time spent on related assignments. That is usually not the case, however.

Another problem associated with the semester killer is that measurement experts advise against making an important decision, such as whether or not a student will pass or fail a course or a grade level, based on any one assessment task. The observed score of even a well-constructed assessment task is a factor of both the true score (the score a student would get if there were no error in measurement) and measurement error. Creating a situation in which success or failure in a course or a grade level could be the result of measurement error risks misrepresenting student performance and penalizing students unfairly.

• • • • • • • • • • • • •

Schools and districts should review their course or subject grading practices to ensure that composite grades reflect the importance of identified and agreed-upon course standards, not time spent on the "semester killer." Such a review may lead to the conclusion that it's time to "kill the killer."

Late Work Not Accepted!

"This assignment is due at 8:00 Tuesday morning. If it is not in at 8:00, you will get a zero in the grade book and we're moving on—late work will not be accepted."

Messages such as this are communicated to students in many classrooms on a daily basis and reflect homework policies in many schools. But do such policies and practices contribute to student learning?

Homework should not be assigned to punish students. Homework should not be assigned as "busywork." Homework should be assigned because the teacher assigning it believes the exercise will advance student mastery of important course or grade-level content and skills. That being the case, homework policies should encourage students to complete all assigned work, even if it is late, because the primary goal is student academic learning, not behavioral compliance with rules and time lines. We would rather have students learn the targeted material a day or two late than not learn it at all.

Plus, it is important to ask whether policies that prohibit late work produce the desired effect—students turning work in and on time. Anecdotal evidence from teachers suggests that students who do not turn assignments in on time are not affected by the threat of a zero. In fact, many of them want to be absolved of the responsibility for completing their work. "I'm fine with a zero—I didn't want to do the work anyway."

The consequence for not doing your work should be that you have to do your work.

That is not to say that there should be no consequences for turning work in late. Most Americans believe schools have a responsibility for teaching students important workplace expectations, including getting one's work done and done on time. But personal responsibility is a behavioral issue and should be dealt with as such. Failure to comply with classroom rules and time lines should result in behavioral consequences (for example, one-on-one conferences, parental intervention, loss of free time and privileges). Failure to turn work in on time should be recorded as part of a work ethic standard and not as part of a course or grade-level content-area standard.

Reasonable Limits and Alternatives

Of course, this position toward late work has practical limits. As with reassessment (discussed in Chapter 2), it is reasonable for teachers to set a date beyond which late work will no longer be accepted, usually at or sometime shortly after the completion of the related unit. At some point the opportunity for genuine learning intended by the assignment expires, and teachers cannot be expected to manage a blizzard of late assignments turned in at the end of the grading period by students interested in points and not learning.

Another modification to the approach to late work proposed here may be needed in cases where students can simply copy the assignment as it is reviewed in class and turn it in late without having really learned anything from it. Sometimes the assignment can be modified to include different tasks that address the same content or skills. The teacher might quiz the student orally to see if he or she really knows what he or she is doing. And some homework assignments simply cannot be made up as originally presented (for example, a field trip). But the concept that should be reflected in homework policies is that as long as students can still learn something by completing the assignment, we want the work turned in.

Although still in its infancy as far as effects on student achievement are concerned, the concept of the flipped classroom offers another promising approach to issues related to homework and homework completion. The idea is that students are introduced to new material at home through podcasts or other technology-enabled delivery systems and then engage in guided and independent practice activities in class.

Homework is for the purposes of practicing skills learned in class or preparation for upcoming classroom instructional activities. Students should not be asked to complete homework that they have not already demonstrated some capacity to do under teacher guidance. The flipped classroom offers opportunities for students to engage in practice and preparation activities with teacher guidance, helping somewhat to level the playing field for students in terms of varying time, support, and access to resources at home.

A common argument against allowing students to turn in work late is that such a practice is not fair to those students who did complete their work on time. Well, what injustices have been done? First, remember that behavioral consequences for not completing work on time are sometimes in order. Also, in schools or districts where policy dictates that work ethic will constitute a specified proportion of final grades for a course or grade-level subject, students who consistently complete their work on time will be rewarded. Finally, unit or topic grades are not at issue here. Homework is a form of formative assessment and as such should not be included in the calculation of final academic topic grades.

Another common argument is "Students won't do the homework if they don't get credit for it." But the fact is that, in most schools, students do get credit for doing homework—something teachers should remind them of on a regular basis. Homework is tied directly to course or grade-level academic goals, as are summative assessments. Students who do their homework will be rewarded in the form of higher scores on summative assessments. If that does not prove to be true in most cases, there is something wrong with the homework assignments, the summative assessment, or the classroom instruction.

"What about the student who does not do her homework and still gets high scores on summative assessments?" Good for her. She is demonstrating good judgment by not doing *that* homework—she does not need to. For her, the assignments would just be busywork. Assignments for such students should be modified to challenge them, and failure to complete those modified assignments should be recorded and reported as work ethic rather than as part of a content or grade-level academic standard.

Another method of reinforcing the timely completion of homework is to periodically administer short comprehension quizzes that sample the content or skill emphasized in the assignment. Students who complete the homework and do well on the quiz receive credit—not for simply doing the work but for understanding the material. Credit awarded in this manner preserves the validity of grades by reflecting demonstrated knowledge and skills, not work ethic. Results also provide teachers and students with information on who needs further instruction. Students who do not do the homework and still score well on the quizzes—not a problem. They know the material, and their grades should reflect that.

Looking Ahead—and Abroad

To the extent that we are focusing on preparing students for college, it is worth pointing out that in most cases college students do not turn in homework at all. Assigning and evaluating homework but not grading it is, in fact, more aligned with college practices than are more punitive homework policies.

International comparisons indicate that teachers in the United States spend too much time and emotional energy fretting over homework and homework completion. Suskind (2012) makes the following observation:

> U.S. teachers lead the charge in making homework a high-stakes event, with nearly 70% selecting to grade homework, compared to 6% in Germany, 14% in Japan, and 28% in Canada, despite research suggesting that grading students on outside work encourages them

to limit their focus, cheat, strive for the minimally set standards of success, and produces undue stress on family dynamics. (p. 53)

I trust readers are aware of how U.S. schools do in international comparisons vis-à-vis the countries in Suskind's study. Maybe it is time to lighten up a bit on the whole homework thing.

Equity, Reliability, and the 10-Minute Rule

Including homework scores in students' academic grades also raises issues related to equity and reliability. Not all students have equal opportunities to complete homework, with students living in poverty having less time and support and fewer resources at home than students from middle- and upper-income families. Is it fair to base students' grades on their parents' shortcomings or society's economic policies?

The reliability of grades is thrown into question when they include homework. Parents are suspected of "helping" children with homework at the elementary level, and students report that copying homework is rampant at the secondary level. Teachers cannot be certain who did work completed outside class and whether or not the student would receive a similar score if assessed under teacher supervision.

Time spent on homework by U.S. students, at least by those who are conscientious about doing their work, is also often out of sync with relevant research. The "10-minute rule," a general guideline suggested by Duke University researcher Harris Cooper (*Duke Today*, 2006) and others, recommends no more than 10 minutes of homework per grade level—1st graders, 10 minutes; 12th graders, 2 hours. Other research supports this recommendation with data indicating that time spent in excess of this guideline is actually counterproductive (Fernández-Alonso, Suárez-Álvarez, & Muñiz, 2015).

• • • • • • • • • • • • • • •

Many of our schools need to examine the purposes of homework, students' ability to do the work, the tendency to make homework a high-stakes event, and the time devoted to homework. Changes may well be in order.

The Illusion of Objectivity

Confronted with the six counterproductive assessment and grading practices discussed thus far (the zero, extra credit, combining academic performance with work ethic and citizenship, averaging, the "semester killer," and not accepting late work), defenders of the status quo respond by playing what they believe is a final trump card. It goes something like this: "Well, I agree you've caused me to question some of my practices, but at least what you call the traditional approach to classroom assessment and grading is objective."

Balderdash! This unfounded belief in the detached, impersonal, and unbiased nature of traditional grading practices is what Madgic (1988) calls the illusion of objectivity.

How Subjectivity Challenges Objectivity

Subjective decisions affect the assessment and grading process in several ways. A few examples illustrate the point.

Guskey (2009) reports on his synthesis of survey data collected over several years regarding the factors teachers include in determining course or subject grades. Among the 18 types of data listed are exams, papers, quizzes, labs, oral presentations, homework completion, and effort. The point (here, at least) is not that some of these frequently used data types are right and some are wrong, but rather that different teachers of the same course or grade level in the same school choose different factors. So if your son is assigned to a class taught by Mr. Smith, who bases grades entirely on exams and papers, his final course grade for the same body of work could be very different than if he had been assigned to Mr. Jones, who includes quizzes and homework completion in final course grades. Sounds pretty subjective.

It gets worse. Even in cases in which grade-level or course teachers get together and agree on which data will be used to determine grades, those teachers often weight those factors differently, thus again introducing subjective decisions into the determination of grades.

In a training session for ASCD's cadre The Art and Science of Teaching, Robert Marzano provided the following example of how subjectivity enters into classroom assessment and grading practices:

> How many points, out of 100, would you assign to each of three sections of an exam?
>
> Section A: Ten items that require the recall of important but *simpler* content that was explicitly taught.
>
> Section B: Four items that ask for application of *complex* content that was explicitly taught and in situations similar to what was taught.
>
> Section C: Two items that ask for application in novel situations that *go beyond* what was explicitly taught.

There are no wrong answers to Marzano's question; it is a matter of individual professional judgment. (You see where this is going, don't you?) One teacher might assign 10, 70, and 20 points (weight) for Sections A, B, and C, respectively, under the philosophy that being able to apply material taught in class is most important, whereas a second teacher might employ a 70, 30, 5 distribution, indicating a belief in the importance of committing facts and details to memory.

To continue this exercise, let us assume that a student gets all of Section A correct, half of the items in Section B correct, and none of the Section C items correct. In one class, the student scores a 45 percent (an *F*), and in the other she scores an 85 percent (a *B*) for the same level of performance. Scores among groups of teachers responding to this example typically range from in the 30s to somewhere in the 80s. Does that sound objective?

It is important to note that teachers making these everyday decisions are not deliberately trying to treat students unfairly. The vast majority of educators are making decisions regarding assessment and grading that they believe are in students' best interests. The problem is that in too many schools, these decisions are made independently and thus vary greatly from teacher to teacher.

Guskey (2013) further debunks the belief in the objectivity of the 100-point (percentage) system:

> Overall, the large number of grade categories in the percentage grading scale and the fine discrimination required in determining the differences among categories allow for the greater influence of subjectivity, more error, and diminished reliability. The increased precision of percentage grades is truly far more imaginary than real. . . . Percentage grading systems that attempt to identify 100 distinct levels of performance distort the precision, objectivity, and reliability of grades. (pp. 70 & 72)

Why is the illusion of objectivity a problem? Because key stakeholders in the education community—including teachers, administrators, parents, and students—use it to defend the status quo and as an excuse not to explore and adopt research-based best practices in classroom assessment and grading. As such, the illusion of objectivity serves as a theory of inaction.

School and district leaders can help strip local stakeholders of the blinders created by the illusion of objectivity by exposing subjective assessment and grading decisions made every day in classrooms throughout the United States. For example, the most involved parents in the community (and the parents most likely to *initially* oppose changes to traditional classroom assessment and grading practices) are often keenly aware of which teachers of a given course or grade level are the "hard" and the "easy" graders. Students, too, particularly at the high school level, share information with one another about which teachers are most likely to give an "easy *A*." Holding focus groups and administering surveys to parents and students can expose subjectivity in the existing system.

As for teacher subjectivity, school leaders could develop their own versions of the Guskey or Marzano activities described above, or they could simply ask course- or grade-alike teachers to score a sample of one another's assessment tasks to see if agreement exists across teachers. Experience suggests that absent extensive interreliability training, scores will differ widely, thus again exposing subjectivity in grading.

Getting teachers to agree that the illusion of objectivity exists usually isn't a hard sell. They know it is the elephant in the room that nobody wants to acknowledge. The challenge is to get the issue on the table for open discussion.

It is important to find the right approach in discussing the subjectivity built into many traditional grading practices. Labeling them as backward or dismissing them as methods employed only by ill-informed teachers who remain stuck in the past is counterproductive. Such an approach comes across as a demeaning personal attack ("What's your problem—you don't care about kids, or you're just stupid?"). Teachers are already doing the best they know how to do, and parents and students are only responding to the ways they have been taught and assessed. A better way to broach the topic is to observe that traditional grading practices have served some students well in the past but that we now have the knowledge to serve all students better.

∙ ∙ ∙ ∙ ∙ ∙ ∙ ∙ ∙ ∙ ∙ ∙ ∙ ∙ ∙ ∙

Addressing counterproductive practices and beliefs in U.S. classrooms, schools, and districts represents a significant move on the continuum of effectiveness in classroom assessment and grading. For those who are ready to continue the journey, Destination 2 is the next stop.

DESTINATION

2

Classroom Assessment and Grading as Components of a Guaranteed and Viable Curriculum

• • • • • • • • • • • • • •

With a thorough understanding of both effective and counterproductive assessment and grading practices under its belt, a district might be ready to move farther along the continuum to a system of assessment and grading grounded in a guaranteed and viable curriculum. As stated in the introduction to this book, a guaranteed and viable curriculum entails identifying a limited number of nonnegotiable topics and corresponding leveled performance expectations for every grading period of every grade-level subject and course. Classroom assessments and instructional materials tied to these topics and performance expectations complete the package. In other words, districts are clear about what students will learn and at what performance levels, no matter which teacher the student has—guaranteed!

Moving to a guaranteed and viable curriculum involves a complex mix of challenging personal beliefs, rethinking instruction, and learning new ways to assess in a standards-based world. It is also a lot of work, much of which must be well under way before teachers are asked to even begin piloting the system.

A district leadership team leading the transition to assessment and grading as components of a guaranteed and viable curriculum must be knowledgeable about the organizational conditions necessary to support and sustain the change and the steps involved in making the transition. Aligning instructional materials to new or revised instructional units is important, as failure to do so adds unnecessary complications and frustration to the transition, negatively affecting teachers' attitudes about the concept itself.

An initial and critical step in the process of developing a guaranteed and viable curriculum is that of identifying measurement topics addressed in major grade- or course-level standards and then creating scoring scales and corresponding leveled assessment tasks that direct and evaluate the related learning. Determining final scores and grades in a way that is consistent and fair to students is critical to successful implementation as well.

Each of these steps takes time, training, resources, and a lot of leadership support. A successful transition to standards-based education and standards-based grading requires specific types of support for teachers from school and district leaders. This leadership imperative requires knowing what support is needed, assessing and developing the capacity to provide that support, and delivering on commitments.

Fortunately, there are schools that have already been down this path. Examining their processes and products can shed light on the work to be done to transition to a sustainable system of grading based on a guaranteed and viable curriculum.

● ● ● ● ● ● ● ● ● ● ● ● ● ●

Organizational Conditions Necessary to Move Beyond Traditional Grading Practices

Earl (2003) describes changing classroom assessment as "the beginning of a revolution—a revolution in classroom practices of all kinds" (p. 15). Certain conditions must be present for any revolution to be successful. Researchers have identified organizational conditions that form the foundation and create the climate for significant change in schools, and school and district leaders contemplating the move to standards-based grading should assess the status of these conditions in their organizations and develop them as needed.

Marzano, Warrick, and Simms (2014) identify five levels of operation schools are advised to intentionally develop to become high-reliability organizations, based on the work of Robert Marzano. The levels complement and correspond with the steps in moving to standards-based education delineated in Chapter 9 of this book. As the term "level" suggests, ascendancy to each level depends on the establishment of the level or levels below.

The first two levels—"Safe and Collaborative Culture" and "Effective Teaching in Every Classroom"—should be well established before attempting to develop a guaranteed and viable curriculum (which is actually Level 3 on Marzano's list). Thus they are pertinent at this point in our discussion.

Level 1: Safe and Collaborative Culture

The professional literature on organizational change is united in the conclusion that for people to fully engage in significant change, they need to feel that it is safe to do a number of things: to take risks, to make mistakes, to fail, to challenge assumptions, and to admit to supervisors their doubts and their need for help. Without a safe school climate, teachers retreat to their classrooms, hunker down, and pretend to implement the change expected by their supervisors. Significant and sustainable change does not typically happen under those conditions.

Likewise, arriving at a common set of values and beliefs about classroom assessment and grading, prioritizing standards, identifying performance expectations, and developing valid and reliable formative and summative assessments are processes and tasks that will not get accomplished in an environment in which teachers and administrators are used to working in isolation. A climate that internalizes collaboration is necessary to get this work done.

What are the characteristics of a collaborative culture, and how does a school move from isolation to collaboration? What obstacles interfere with efforts to establish a collaborative school environment, and how are new hires selected for and acclimated to a school culture organized around principles of collaboration?

Schools with collaborative cultures share several characteristics, including

- A common vision and agreed-upon outcomes for student learning and performance.

- Shared core values.

- A common framework for effective teaching, or what some researchers call a common language of instruction (more on this in the next section).

- Shared responsibility for student learning.

- Trust.

- Effective communication and openness.

- Respect for differences.

- Efficacy, or a belief in the collective ability of the faculty and staff to realize the school's vision and desired student learning outcomes.

Schools with collaborative cultures focus on learning—student *and* adult learning. Collaborative cultures cannot be mandated. Instead, there exists a voluntary effort to seek self-improvement through teamwork. Teachers are partners in making decisions and in identifying and designing professional development opportunities, and in return they share responsibility with administrators for quality control with regard to classroom instruction and assessment of student learning. In schools with collaborative cultures, the primary purpose of teacher evaluation is growth, not accountability, and teachers model that same ethos in their work with students.

Of course, a school's move from a culture of isolation to one of collaboration is not immediately embraced by everyone on the faculty. Many veteran teachers have become comfortable in the safety of a "my classroom is my kingdom" environment. (I have at times defined a high school as a collection of educational entrepreneurs held together by a common parking lot.) In such environments, a lack of trust and common purpose, ineffective communication, and administrators' need to consolidate power present formidable obstacles to collaboration.

School structures, or a lack thereof, can also present obstacles to collaboration. Some schools talk the collaborative culture talk but provide no time for teachers to collaborate. Absent established protocols and leadership training, collaborative groups can quickly become dysfunctional and counterproductive. Having no common model of effective instruction makes sharing responsibility for student learning and self-improvement through teamwork all but impossible.

Perhaps the most damaging obstacle to establishing a culture of collaboration is a lack of modeling by the school principal and leadership team. Trust, open and effective communication, a respect for differences, and a belief in the power of shared leadership start at the top. Administrators, walk the walk.

In addition to modeling, necessary steps in establishing a collaborative school culture include involving the school community in establishing a school vision and set of shared values and working with the faculty to establish a framework for effective instruction. Shared student achievement goals also build community. School structures, including the school schedule, must be designed to facilitate collaboration. A clear purpose and expected outcomes as well as leadership training for collaborative groups must be established.

At Klein Forest High School in Klein, Texas, data teams led by teacher team leaders who are coached by designated building administrators meet weekly to discuss student performance and plan instruction. Data teams at James Campbell High School in Hawaii meet regularly under the direction of team leaders to discuss the results of common formative assessments and to plan accordingly. Teachers at Kohala Middle School and Kohala High School, also in Hawaii, are provided with periodic released time during the school day to work by department on 6–12 articulation.

Not every teacher candidate possesses a collaborative mindset. Even new faculty members who *do* possess such a mindset can find the structures, values, norms, and protocols of an established collaborative school culture bewildering. During the hiring process, care must be taken to identify, through reference checks and interview questions, a candidate's past behaviors with regard to collaboration. Equally important, interviewers must make clear to teacher candidates the collaborative behaviors expected at the school. For potential hires, the message should be "Buyer beware: if you want to be left alone to do your own thing, this is not the place for you."

After a teacher has been hired, administrators, team leaders, department chairs, and teacher coaches play key roles in acclimating him or her to the school culture. During preservice days and the first two years of employment, new hires must be given the time and structures needed to learn and become comfortable with how the school functions. School leadership must commit to helping new teachers become contributing members of the team.

A myriad of surveys and protocols are available for formally assessing school and district climate, but frankly, this is not rocket science. Visitors to a school or district can quickly assess the extent to which faculty and staff members feel it is safe to take risks and express opinions. Union representatives know. School leaders should know, too. If they do not, that says more about the school's culture than any survey results would.

Sometimes, school leaders believe that they have a firm grasp of the school culture and that that culture is highly functional—but their perceptions are incorrect. For this reason, I advise periodically administering a research-based, comprehensive school climate survey. The National School Climate Center (http://www.schoolclimate.org/climate/practice.php) and ASCD (http://www.ascd.org/professional-development/school-climate-and-culture-resources.aspx) are two of several organizations that offer climate survey services. Leaders might also contact their professional organizations (the National Association of Elementary School Principals, the Association for Middle Level Education, the National Association of Secondary School Principals, or the School Superintendents Association) as well as their state departments of education for information on school climate surveys. Some organizations, such as the North Dakota Lead Center, offer customizable online surveys (http://www.ndlead.k12.nd.us/surveys/listofsurvey/SAtools/SCtools.html).

Administering a school climate or collaborative culture survey must be followed up with a collaborative analysis of results by a team representative of the school community. If students and parents were involved in taking the survey, they should also be involved in analyzing the results. Major conclusions from the survey analysis should be shared with appropriate stakeholders, along with action steps and monitoring strategies for areas in need of improvement. Action steps may be included in school strategic or improvement plans.

Safe and collaborative school cultures don't happen automatically. They are the result of deliberate, planned, and monitored action on the part of the school's leadership team.

Level 2: Effective Teaching in Every Classroom

In this section I am referring to the well-researched finding that variations in student achievement are greater across classrooms within a school than across schools. Michael Fullan (2006) is among the many researchers and writers who have chronicled the vast differences in expectations and effectiveness, and therefore in student achievement, among teachers in schools. Effective teaching in every classroom assumes a school or district has collaboratively adopted a model or framework for effective teaching that serves as a common language of instruction. Without a common language, we cannot have a conversation about teaching and learning, about classroom assessment and grading, or about much of anything else. Without conversation there is no systemic improvement. And as Sir Michael Barber and Mona Mourshed (2007) pointed out several years ago, "The quality of an education system cannot exceed the quality of its teachers" (p. 16).

Several research-based frameworks are available for adaptation and adoption (see, for example, Danielson, 2007; Fisher & Frey, 2008; Marzano, 2007; and Reeves, 2008b). The important point is not *which* framework is chosen but rather that there is one, that it is well understood by teachers and administrators in the school or district, and that it helps guide all decisions with regard to teaching and learning—hiring, professional development, materials selection, teacher evaluation, budgeting, and so on.

The adoption and institutionalization of a common language of instruction, and the use of that language in the context of a safe and collaborative culture to ensure effective teaching in every classroom, rests squarely on the shoulders of building and district leaders—administrators and teacher leaders. So the question becomes, if someone were to ask teachers in your school or district what model of effective teaching the organization embraces, and what the major tenets of that model are, could they respond convincingly?

• • • • • • • • • • • • • •

A school district that can demonstrate a safe, collaborative culture and effective teaching is in a position to move to establishing a guaranteed and viable curriculum as a basis for classroom assessment and grading. Without these two conditions in place, the district needs to lay further groundwork before proceeding.

Steps in Moving to a Guaranteed and Viable Curriculum

Creating a "pedagogical infrastructure" to support a system of classroom assessment and grading based on a guaranteed and viable curriculum takes time, expertise, and resources—all three of which usually take money. The work is most often done by grade-level or subject-area teams of teachers and specialists (curriculum coordinators, instructional coaches, subject-area experts, assessment specialists) and can easily take more than a year to accomplish. The process of building a standards-based education infrastructure must be completed before teachers are asked to implement new grading practices in their classrooms. Building a standards-based infrastructure is part of an overall implementation plan, which is discussed in Chapter 13.

Districts—especially smaller ones—often need outside technical expertise to build local capacity in areas such as unpacking standards, developing measurement topics and scoring scales, creating valid and reliable assessment tasks, and assessing IT compatibility. Simply assuming that rank-and-file teachers have the necessary skills usually results in disaster.

Starting from Scratch with State or Common Core Standards

The building blocks of a guaranteed and viable curriculum are state standards, measurement topics, scoring scales, and formative and summative assessment tasks. Figure 9.1 outlines a conceptually simple but logistically, technically, and emotionally complex process for turning these building blocks into a solid infrastructure for standards-based education.

This fairly straightforward process presumes a district is developing instructional units from scratch, starting with state standards. It begins with unpacking grade-level or course standards to identify essential elements and then organizing those elements into measurement topics. Scoring scales that describe the performance expected of students at different levels of proficiency—for example, basic, proficient, and advanced—are developed for each measurement topic, and formative and summative assessment tasks are written for each corresponding proficiency level. Finally, instructional materials are aligned to the appropriate instructional units.

FIGURE 9.1

Steps to Creating a Guaranteed and Viable Curriculum Based on State Standards

1. Unpack state standards to identify essential elements.

2. Organize related essential elements into measurement topics.

3. Design a scoring scale for each measurement topic.

4. Use the scoring scale to design formative and summative assessments.

5. Organize measurement topics into instructional units.

6. Align instructional materials with standards-based instructional units.

March and Peters (2015) suggest a similar set of steps when developing instructional units around Common Core standards:

- Examine the Common Core standards and thus define what students will do to demonstrate mastery and what strategies teachers will use to help students construct meaning;

- Thoughtfully cluster the standards into chunks that address a unifying theme or topic that provides a life context in which to address the cluster of standards;

- Develop course tools for classroom use, such as pacing guides, curriculum maps, or unit plans that actually guide each teacher's daily classroom instruction; and

- Devise common, standards-based assessments at each grade level to continuously monitor student performance and to provide timely and specific intervention to each student. (p. 65)

Although the process itself is not difficult to comprehend, carrying it out is time-consuming, technically challenging, and emotionally charged. Strongly held philosophical and personal differences among teachers come to the surface as they prioritize standards, decide which essential elements fit into which measurement topics and which measurement topics should be combined into a single instructional unit, and decide what students should be expected to know and do at each performance level of each measurement topic. Developing scoring scales and writing valid and reliable assessment tasks require considerable technical expertise. All of the tasks in this process take time.

Expecting teams of teachers to accomplish this work during regular grade-level or department meetings is unrealistic. Schools and districts address the issues of time and expertise in a variety of ways. To provide the time needed to transition to a system of classroom assessment and grading based on a guaranteed and viable curriculum, schools may offer released time for grade-level or department teams, paid summer work for development teams, or data team or professional learning time, or they may form district curriculum leader teams. In the high school where I was principal for many years, we were able to free up a teacher part-time for a semester to develop some of this work.

Schools and districts also provide technical expertise in a variety of ways. Larger districts often have technical expertise in house, and smaller districts in most states can access technical expertise through area education agencies, regional or state departments of education, or Boards of Cooperative Educational Services. Some schools and districts elect to train a cadre of teachers and administrators to provide the technical expertise needed. Both nonprofit and for-profit organizations, such as ASCD and Marzano Research Laboratory, offer technical services relative to the demands presented here. And, of course, countless independent consultants—some qualified and some not—can be contracted for services.

Starting with Existing Instructional Units in Mind

Experience in the field suggests that districts do not typically start the standards-based development process with state standards in isolation because teachers are already heavily invested in units of instruction that they are reluctant to abandon. Using existing instructional units as part of the development process is much more palatable to teachers. Figure 9.2 outlines a development process that uses existing instructional products. Let's take a closer look at each step in the process.

Unpacking State Standards to Identify Essential Elements

The first step of this process involves unpacking (if necessary), combining, and eliminating standards or elements of standards. Many standards contain two or more components or elements that, although related and perhaps taught together, address different knowledge or skill sets and therefore constitute individual measurement topics. Chappuis (2014) provides the following example of a single standard (Grade 6, Writing Standard 8 of the Common Core State Standards) with at least four separate skill sets:

> Gather relevant information from multiple print and digital sources; assess the credibility of each source; and quote or paraphrase the data and conclusions of others while avoiding plagiarism and providing basic bibliographic information for sources. (p. 21)

FIGURE 9.2

Creating a Guaranteed and Viable Curriculum Based on Existing Units of Instruction

1. Unpack state standards to identify essential elements.

2. Examine existing instructional units (based on district curricula) and identify the standards or essential elements that are or could be legitimately addressed.

3. Organize related essential elements into measurement topics as needed.

4. Design a scoring scale for each measurement topic.

5. Use the scoring scale to design formative and summative assessments.

6. Identify priority standards and elements not addressed and design or modify units accordingly.

7. Align instructional materials with standards-based instructional units.

Standards must be unpacked to identify these elements, and teachers will need to decide where, if at all, each element fits in the planned instructional sequence.

Once teachers have identified the relevant standards and elements, their next task is to decide which elements are essential, which elements can be combined, and which elements must be eliminated from further development. Suggesting that standards or essential elements of standards be prioritized and that only high-priority standards or elements be selected for development using the seven-step process outlined in Figure 9.2 recognizes that there is simply not enough time in the school year to develop a deep understanding of all recommended grade-level or course standards. Heflebower, Hoegh, and Warrick (2014) suggest the following criteria for selecting high-priority standards:

1. Endurance—Knowledge and skills that will last beyond a class period or course.

2. Leverage—Knowledge and skills that cross over into many domains of learning.

3. Readiness—Knowledge and skills important to subsequent content or courses.

4. Teacher judgment—Knowledge of content area and ability to identify more- and less-important content.

5. Assessment—Student opportunity to learn content that will be assessed. (p. 18)

What about the remaining standards? Some will merit limited exposure, primarily because state tests will call for at least a superficial knowledge of the content embodied in them. Some simply should and must be ignored. Less is more.

Educators can turn to various resources for help in prioritizing standards. For example, an excellent resource for K–8 mathematics is Achieve the Core, which lists prioritized standards by grade level (http:// achievethecore.org/content/upload/Focus%20in%20Math_091013_ FINAL.pdf). Between five to eight priority standards—manageable numbers—are identified for each grade level.

Examining Existing Units to Identify Relevant Standards or Essential Elements

Step 2 capitalizes on development work already done on grade-level or course standards by using existing units of instruction whenever possible, revising as necessary. Standards are not new to education, and in many cases veteran teachers have already devoted time and energy to producing sound units of instruction. Totally discarding that work and starting over from scratch is a waste of capital and demoralizes teachers.

For example, a group of high school biology teachers I worked with had long been teaching units on genetics, sexual and asexual reproduction, and inherited traits. They discovered that with a few modifications those units could be combined to address the standard "Explore reproduction and the transfer of genetic material in living things." In another case, a family and consumer sciences teacher was able to modify lessons on stages of child development and birth defects to address elements of local standards on pregnancy and childbirth. Existing instructional units should be examined to determine which standards or elements of standards are addressed in them or could be legitimately addressed with modification.

Organizing Essential Elements into Measurement Topics

Step 3 directs us to organize related essential elements into measurement topics, as needed. Measurement topics form the foundation for the scoring scales developed in the next stage of the process. A measurement topic should consist of standards or elements of standards that are related. The concept of *covariance* is often used to describe this relationship. Covariance means that as proficiency increases for element A, so does proficiency for element B. Students cannot learn more about element A without also learning more about element B. Elements related in this way are taught and assessed together. The cell-division processes of mitosis and meiosis might serve as examples. Some units of instruction may already be structured around a single measurement topic, therefore making this step unnecessary.

Like standards, the number of measurement topics selected for inclusion in any one grade level or course must be limited. Fifteen measurement topics with corresponding scoring scales and sets of leveled assessment tasks for a yearlong course would allow teachers to spend an average of at least two weeks per goal, which is enough time to deliver and evaluate cognitively demanding instruction. Figure 9.3 offers examples of measurement topics.

Designing Scoring Scales

Building a guaranteed and viable curriculum gets more difficult at Step 4—designing scoring scales. Marzano (2006) recommends the generic template in Figure 9.4 as the basis for the development of scoring scales.

FIGURE 9.3
Examples of Measurement Topics

Math 7

- Real numbers
- Percentages and proportions
- Data analysis
- Spatial geometry
- Coordinate geometry
- Algebra

Instrumental Music

- Performance
- Participation
- Literacy and application

Reading (from CCSS.ELA-LITERACY.RL)

- Key ideas and details
- Craft and structure
- Integration of knowledge and ideas
- Range of Reading and level of Text Complexity

Begin the process of writing a scoring scale for a particular measurement topic by identifying what students are expected to demonstrate that they know and can do at Level 3 of the template. Level 3 defines proficiency or grade-level expectations for the topic and is the target for all students. Level 3 should ask students to function at the Application level or above on Bloom's taxonomy or at Levels 2 and 3 on Webb's Depth of Knowledge (DOK) matrix.

Tackle Level 2 of the template next. Level 2 describes an understanding of the more basic knowledge and skills embodied by the measurement topic. Level 2 knowledge and skills often form the building blocks of the performances expected at Level 3 and should target the

FIGURE 9.4

Scoring Scale Template

Topic Score on Scale	Description of Place on Scale
4.0	**In addition to Score 3.0 performance, in-depth inferences and applications that go beyond what was taught**
3.5	In addition to Score 3.0 performance, partial success at inferences and applications that go beyond what was taught
3.0	**No major errors or omissions regarding any of the information and/or processes (simple or complex) that were explicitly taught**
2.5	No major errors or omissions regarding the simpler details and process and partial knowledge of the more complex ideas and processes
2.0	**No major errors or omissions regarding the simpler details and processes but major errors or omissions regarding the more complex ideas and processes**
1.5	Partial knowledge of the simpler details and processes but major errors or omissions regarding the more complex ideas and procedures
1.0	**With help, a partial understanding of some of the simpler details and processes and some of the more complex ideas and processes**
0.5	With help, a partial understanding of some of the simpler details and processes but not the more complex ideas and processes
0.0	**Even with help, no understanding or skill demonstrated**

Source: From *Classroom Assessment & Grading That Work* (p. 50), by Robert J. Marzano, 2006, Alexandria, VA: ASCD. Reprinted with permission.

Knowledge and Comprehension levels of Bloom's taxonomy and DOK Levels 1 and 2.

Finally, identify what Level 4 of the generic scoring scale template—"advanced" or "exceeds grade-level expectations"—looks like for the targeted grade level and measurement topic. As the template indicates, Level 4 calls for student performances that demonstrate in-depth inferences and applications that go beyond what was explicitly taught in class. Level 4 often asks students to apply learning in novel situations, and it targets Application and above on Bloom's taxonomy and Webb's DOK Levels 3 and 4.

Figure 9.5 provides an example of a completed scoring scale for the measurement topic "Ecology." The scale was developed by a teacher in Omaha, Nebraska, and follows the design outlined in the Marzano template in Figure 9.4. Some writers advocate letting individual teachers determine Level 4 expectations, thus allowing teachers to put their unique stamp on the process. However, surveys of teachers from schools engaged in the development process suggest a preference for collaboratively defining Level 4.

Scoring scales for a variety of topics and grade levels are available online from measurement experts and school districts that have already engaged in this step of the development process. The Solon (Iowa) Community School District and the Marzano Research Laboratory (http://www.marzano research.com/resources/proficiency-scale-bank) are just two examples.

Using Scoring Scales to Design Valid and Reliable Assessments

Perhaps the most challenging and time-consuming step in the process of developing standards-based education is that of creating valid and reliable formative and summative assessment tasks that evaluate student achievement at Levels 2 through 4 of the scoring scale for each unit.

Looking again at Figure 9.5, assessment tasks must be developed that reveal whether or not students have Level 2 knowledge and skills in order

FIGURE 9.5

Scoring Scale for the Measurement Topic "Ecology"

Advanced Score 4.0	In addition to the Proficient (3.0) performance, makes inferences and extended applications of learning; may include connections to experiences outside coursework.	Ecosystems	**Students will be able to . . .** • Design organisms that can live in multiple biomes.
		Human effect	• Predict how the removal/addition of humans would change the impact of nature on different environments.
		Organism responses	• Synthesize a solution to a lack of internal regulators.
	Proficient + Score 3.5	In addition to the Proficient (3.0) performance, shows partial success at making inferences and extended applications of learning, including connections to outside coursework experiences.	
Proficient Score 3.0	No major errors or omissions regarding any of the information or processes (simple or complex) that were explicitly taught.	Ecosystems	**Students will be able to . . .** • Analyze biomes, including trophic levels, in relation to geographic regions. • Model how the distribution and abundance of different organisms in ecosystems are limited by the availability of matter and energy.
		Human effect	• Evaluate the impacts of human actions and natural causes on Earth's resources (groundwater, rivers, land, fossil fuels).
		Organism responses	• Analyze how organisms adapt to survive due to external and internal changes.
	Basic + Score 2.5	No major errors or omissions regarding any of the information or simpler details and processes (Basic 2.0) and partial knowledge of the more complex ideas and processes (Proficient 3.0).	

FIGURE 9.5
Scoring Scale for the Measurement Topic "Ecology" (continued)

Basic Score 2.0	No major errors or omissions regarding the simpler details and processes, but major errors or omissions regarding the more complex ideas and processes.	Ecosystems	**Students will be able to . . .**
			 • Recall vocabulary (*birth/ death rate, carrying capacity, immigration/emigration*).
			 • Identify all the components of the major biochemical cycles in the biosphere.
			 • Connect the stability of an ecosystem with biological diversity.
			 • Illustrate natural influences (Earth's rotation, mountain ranges, oceans, differential heating) on global climate.
			 • Perform basic processes, such as . . .
			     o Illustrating the uniqueness of each biome.
			     o Organizing organisms in each trophic level.
			     o Classifying factors as biotic or abiotic.
			     o Explaining factors affecting population.

		Human effect	• Recall vocabulary (*renewable/nonrenewable resource, biodegradable, recycling*).
			 • Perform basic processes, such as . . .
			     o Identifying human activities that impact the environment.
			     o Providing alternative options for each negative human impact.

(Continues on next page)

FIGURE 9.5

Scoring Scale for the Measurement Topic "Ecology" (continued)

		Organism responses	• Recall vocabulary (*homeostasis, stimuli, response*).
			• Outline how an organism responds to internal and external changes to survive.
			• Perform basic processes, such as . . .
			    ◦ Showing the process of homeostasis.
			    ◦ Listing stimulus and response pairings.

Below Basic Score 1.0			Partial understanding of some of the simpler details and processes (Basic 2.0) and major errors regarding the more complex ideas and processes (3.0).
Failing Score 0			No evidence or insufficient evidence of student learning.

Source: Copyright 2016 by Jaynie E. Bird. Used with permission.

for a teacher to make decisions about student learning, both during and at the conclusion of instruction. The same is true for content and skills at Levels 3 and 4. Imagine, then, a comprehensive summative assessment for a unit of instruction based on two measurement topics and corresponding scoring scales. That summative assessment must include six sets of assessment items or tasks—sets of items or tasks for Levels 2, 3, and 4 for each of the two measurement topics. Let's take a look at examples from various subject areas at the high school level.

Math

Level 2:

1. Identify the degree of this polynomial and classify it by its number of items: $3x^2 - 2x - 8$
2. Is -4 a solution to $-8 \le 3x + 5$?

Level 3:

1. Factor completely: $3x^2 - 2x - 8$
2. Solve this inequality and graph its solution on a number line: $-8 \leq 3x + 5$

Level 4:

1. Given that $(x + 2)$ is a factor of $x^3 - 5x^2 - 2x + 24$, factor the polynomial completely.
2. Describe a situation from business, industry, sports, entertainment, or a similar field where inequalities could be used to model a method of solution.

English/Language Arts

Level 2:

1. How would you define "relationship"? "Love"?
2. How would you describe the relationship between the Capulets and the Montagues?
3. How does the balcony scene begin?

Level 3:

1. Create a picture to illustrate the relationship between the Capulets and the Montagues.
2. What qualities do you see in Romeo and Juliet's relationship?
3. In what ways are the two families similar? Different?

Level 4:

1. What would have happened if the couple had not married in secret?
2. If Romeo and Juliet had not died, would the families' relationship be better or worse? Explain your answer.
3. What might you say about groups/families that have been feuding/not getting along?

Science

Level 2:

1. What are the substances formed in a chemical reaction called?
2. Identify the two subatomic particles in the nucleus.

Level 3:

1. How does the development of the atomic model compare to the development of other scientific models?
2. Compare and contrast cations and anions.

Level 4:

You are an environmental toxicologist and the local authorities have called on you to investigate the potential effects of a spill on the highway. Two semis, one hauling sodium carbonate and one hauling acetic acid, collided. The chemicals appear to be reacting, and authorities are concerned that the by-products might be harmful. Perform a controlled experiment with these two chemicals to determine the potential impact on the surrounding area. Write a report explaining the results of your experiment to authorities.

Information Technology

Level 2: What symbol represents an absolute cell reference?

Level 3: How would you create an absolute cell reference?

Level 4: As data are added, would it be more effective to manually manipulate a spreadsheet or to use absolute cell references? Explain your answer.

Business

Level 2: List the steps of the accounting cycle.

Level 3: Analyze what makes a financial company healthy.

Level 4: Review financial statements (assets, liabilities, capital, revenue, and expenses) to determine the health of a company. Make a recommendation as to whether or not to invest in this company. Defend your answer.

Family and Consumer Sciences

Level 2:

Match the kind of knife with its intended use:

___ Paring	a. Cuts through bone
___ Chef's	b. Separates meat from bone
___ Serrated	c. Slices bread
___ Cleaver	d. Peels potatoes

Level 3:

Skill demonstration: While under teacher direction, the student will cut potatoes or carrots to industry standards using safety and sanitation procedures and proper motion and knife-handling techniques. The cuts will include rondell, medium and large dice, and mince.

Level 4:

Given a vegetable and a scenario for use, the student will prepare a vegetable using the most appropriate knife cut and industry standards. The student will also demonstrate correct procedures for safety and sanitation and proper motion and knife-handling techniques.

A table of specifications such as the one in Figure 9.6 that depicts an instructional unit with four measurement topics can help ensure that all the assessment bases are covered. In this example, a teacher or team of teachers is planning for and developing formative and summative assessment tasks for a unit of instruction that addresses four topics. To gather data on student performance levels on all four topics, all cells in the table must have entries—that is, assessment tasks must be developed for each level of each topic. If, for example, the cell for Level 4 of Measurement Topic 2 is empty, there will be no way of knowing if students can perform

FIGURE 9.6
Table of Specifications for Standards-Based Education

	Level 2	Level 3	Level 4
Measurement Topic 1			
Measurement Topic 2			
Measurement Topic 3			
Measurement Topic 4			

at that level on that topic. Placing item numbers or simply putting checkmarks in the cells of the table as tasks are developed serves as a safeguard against missing performance data.

Of course, it is not necessary that every instance of formative and summative assessment evaluate every level of every unit measurement topic. Especially in the case of formative assessment, teachers may want to evaluate just one or two aspects of the learning progression—for example, just Level 2 knowledge of one of the unit measurement topics. What is important is that at some point during the unit, all levels of all measurement topics are evaluated for both formative and summative purposes.

Assessment tasks need not all be newly constructed. Existing items and tasks can often serve as a starting point for building unit packages for formative and summative assessment that meet the criteria outlined here.

In addition to the need for each unit assessment package to be comprehensive—assessing Levels 2 through 4 of each unit measurement topic—assessment tasks should be *valid* and *reliable*. It is important to understand what these terms mean.

Validity has to do with the degree to which assessment tasks evaluate student performance on the targeted content and skills and nothing else. Lack of proficiency in writing in English, a missing name on a paper, difficulty following directions, and rewards for unused bathroom passes erode validity. Including items or tasks on assessments that ask students to recall information only tangentially related to the targeted content and skills is a frequent cause of validity problems. A simple check for validity is to ask a colleague to look at your assessments and scoring scales. Can he or she match the assessment items with the content and skills identified in the unit measurement topic scoring scales? "Leftover" assessment tasks—those that are not matched to unit content or skills—should be discarded.

Reliability addresses the question, "Will my assessment always yield the same results?" Homework is often an unreliable assessment of

knowledge and skills. Students who complete their homework satis-
factorily, perhaps with help from parents or classmates, may perform
poorly on in-class assessments over the same material. Another source
of reliability problems has to do with evaluator influence, bias, or error.
Have a colleague who teaches the same class score several of your assessments to see if the results are the same as when you scored them.

Formative assessment is an essential component of standards-based
education and, by definition, includes feedback to students and teachers based on assessment results. Educators are, for the most part, keenly
aware of the importance of soliciting feedback regarding student learning
during the learning process in order to make adjustments to instruction
before moving on in cases where the evidence suggests learning has fallen
short of the level necessary for future success. Carefully constructed formative assessment activities are an essential tool for gathering feedback
for learning.

The effects of feedback for impact can be greatly increased by adher-
ing to the following five guiding principles, which are supported by both
research and practitioner experience.

GUIDING PRINCIPLE #1

**Feedback for impact is targeted at key subskills and bodies of
enabling knowledge (building blocks) in the learning progression.** James Popham (2008) is among the many researchers who
emphasize the importance of identifying the key building blocks in
a learning progression in order to direct instruction at those foundational skills and bodies of knowledge that students must attain to
accomplish the targeted learning goal. If the "big picture" curricular
goal in a history class is to develop a well-crafted argumentative essay
on whether or not the George W. Bush administration was planning to
go to war against Saddam Hussein before the 2001 attack on the World
Trade Center, students will need content knowledge about the Persian

Gulf War of 1991 and skills in organizing content before beginning to formulate their essays.

Once a particular subskill or body of knowledge has been identified as essential to success, it follows that moving on with instruction without evidence that students have mastered the knowledge or skill is likely to result in little more than frustration and a reduction in students' sense of efficacy. Classroom formative assessment provides that evidence.

📍 GUIDING PRINCIPLE #2

Feedback for impact targets those concepts and skills that students typically find difficult or harbor misconceptions about. Experienced teachers can often predict the points in the learning progression at which students typically experience difficulty or express misconceptions. For example, students (and adults) often think mass and weight are the same thing. A teacher needs to correct this misconception before the 3rd grade science unit on measurement progresses very far. It is only prudent to profit from experience and plan formative assessment tasks to confirm or refute such predictions before moving on.

📍 GUIDING PRINCIPLE #3

Feedback for impact aligns with the content included in related classroom and common summative assessments. This principle speaks to the importance of alignment between what is taught and assessed at the classroom level and what is assessed by state common assessments (e.g., PARCC, SBAC, Iowa Assessments, Florida State Assessments). The content assessed by classroom formative and summative assessments must be the content sampled by state common assessments if students are expected to perform well on those assessments.

GUIDING PRINCIPLE #4

Feedback for impact includes the levels of cognitive rigor featured in summative assessments. Feedback for impact produces not only evidence of student knowledge and performance of content and skills but also evidence that students can function at the level of cognitive complexity expected of them on later summative assessments. Therefore, formative assessment tasks must include the levels of cognitive complexity students will see later on if such tasks are to serve students and teachers well during instruction.

Students shouldn't see cognitively complex tasks for the first time on either classroom tests or common summative exams, and it is important to remember that cognitive complexity is not the same as task difficulty. Webb's Depth of Knowledge (DOK) instrument is an excellent tool for evaluating the cognitive complexity of classroom formative (and summative) assessment tasks.

Teachers can be invited to bring a typical classroom summative assessment and related formative assessment items from a recently taught unit of instruction to a professional learning community (PLC) session for collaborative analyses of cognitive rigor using Webb's tool. Revising classroom assessments can then become the PLC's work if the level of complexity identified falls short of state or local expectations.

GUIDING PRINCIPLE #5

Feedback for impact mirrors the format of the items included in summative assessments. For example, if the common summative assessment requires students to use specific computer applications and procedures (drag and drop, highlighting, drawing evidence from multiple resources, constructing graphs, etc.), classroom formative assessments should do so as well. Training in assessment format is probably the only strictly test-prep instruction that is defensible, because the validity of assessment results is eroded when students miss items owing to unfamiliarity with the format rather than lack of content knowledge or skill.

Not all feedback results in improved learning by students. Feedback that affects learning is planned in alignment with research-based guidelines for effectiveness. Feedback without impact is, of course, a colossal waste of time, and no one in the profession today has time to waste.

Feedback for impact in the classroom is more successful when effective feedback has been modeled for teachers during their own learning experiences. Therefore, district and building leaders should adhere to the guiding principles just described when introducing them to classroom teachers. It would be a mistake, for example, to assume that most teachers know how to develop a learning progression, determine the cognitive complexity of standards and assessments, or construct valid and reliable classroom assessments. Planning for professional learning for the first of these topics should include the development of a topic learning progression and the identification of key building blocks and predictable "sticking points" or misconceptions—all informed and supported by aligned formative assessment activities undertaken by teachers throughout the learning experience.

Identifying Standards and Elements Not Addressed and Modifying Units Accordingly

Creating a guaranteed and viable curriculum starting with existing units of instruction leaves open the possibility—or, more likely, the probability—that important elements of priority standards have been left out. This step of the process calls for development teams to identify exactly where (in which grade-level or course topic or topics) each of the essential elements identified in Step 1 of the process is addressed. Missing essential elements can be accounted for either by developing a new unit or by adding topics (with corresponding rubrics and assessment tasks) to existing units of instruction.

Aligning Materials with Standards-Based Instructional Units

The final step in the process of developing a guaranteed and viable curriculum is to align instructional materials with newly created or revised standards-based units of instruction. Field experience in making the move to standards-based education reveals that stress related to the transition is often unnecessarily increased because of a failure to attend to this step in the development process.

Textbooks offer a good starting point. Which sections of the textbook support each level of the scoring scale for each topic of the course or grade level? Which sections don't fit at all and should be skipped altogether? Figure 9.7 shows an example of a materials-alignment tool from Heflebower and colleagues (2014). Other materials, such as tutorials, videos, websites, and guest speakers, can also be identified and aligned to the levels on course or grade-level scoring scales.

FIGURE 9.7

Example of a Materials-Alignment Tool

	Scale 1: Slope, distance, and equation of line	Scale 2: Function evaluation	Scale 3: Reasonable graph or graphic representation	Scale 4: Graphing equations	Scale 5: Quadratics
Chapter	Chapter 1 (pages 38–45)				
Score 4.0	pages 43–45				
Score 3.0	pages 40–42				
Score 2.0	pages 38–39				

Source: From *A School Leader's Guide to Standards-Based Grading* (p. 34), by Tammy Heflebower, Jan K. Hoegh, and Phil Warrick, 2014, Bloomington, IN: Marzano Research Laboratory. Copyright 2014 by Marzano Research Laboratory. Reprinted with permission.

•   •   •   •   •   •   •   •   •   •   •   •   •   •

This chapter is designed to walk you through the steps of moving to a system of classroom assessment and grading based on a guaranteed and viable curriculum. Each step is critical, and each step requires considerable time and technical expertise to bring to fruition. As Chapter 13 explains in detail, it is not unusual for districts to spend three or four years and significant resources getting to this point.

The good news is that the fruits of this labor are many. Engaging a faculty and staff in the six-step development process outlined here brings to the forefront instructional and assessment issues crucial to maximizing student learning—issues that have been on the back burner for too long. Doing this work helps to further both individual professional growth and school improvement.

A Look at a Standards-Based Unit of Instruction

Appendix A provides two examples of what it looks like when scoring scales and leveled assessment tasks are packaged together. The algebra unit of instruction consists of two measurement topics (called "learning goals" on the scoring scale) and corresponding leveled summative assessment tasks, whereas the family and consumer sciences unit on birth defects addresses just one measurement topic.

This chapter aims to provide a clear picture of what a unit of instruction looks like when the six-step process outlined in Chapter 9 is employed with fidelity, with an emphasis on designing a scoring scale for a standards-based measurement topic and using that scale to design summative assessment tasks. Consider the following as you examine the examples in Appendix A.

The content and skills detailed for the Basic, Proficient, and Advanced levels of the scoring scales. The performances identified in all three scoring scales include both content and skills and offer enough detail to clarify for students the work to be done and for teachers the instructional strategies and assessment tasks that need to be developed. These performance descriptors serve as the basis for teacher feedback to students as well as student self-assessment and progress monitoring ("Based on this quiz, which Proficient descriptors do you believe you have not yet mastered? What strategies might you try to learn the missing material before the next quiz?").

Notice also the cognitive demand of what students are being asked to demonstrate at the different levels of the scale. At the Basic level, students are primarily being asked to identify, recognize, name, and recall—tasks at the Remembering and Understanding levels on Bloom's taxonomy and Levels 1 and 2 on Webb's Depth of Knowledge (DOK) matrix. Proficient performances, on the other hand, require students to apply, compare and contrast, analyze, justify, solve, write, and determine—tasks at the Applying, Analyzing, and Evaluating levels on Bloom's taxonomy and Level 3 on Webb's DOK matrix. At the Advanced level, students are asked not only to apply, analyze, evaluate, and create but also to do so with tasks that are cognitively demanding (DOK Levels 3 and 4)—for example, "Develop a bill to protect the rights of unborn children from environmental birth defects" and "Create a real-life situation, with the variable expression that models it, and represent the expression in a function table."

Students enrolled in a district using these scoring scales are exposed to the same content and skills and held to the same performance standards regardless of the teacher or school to which they are assigned—a guaranteed and viable curriculum. Scoring scales can be posted online to inform parents of what's expected of their children in school and be used to guide discussion at parent-student-teacher conferences.

The alignment between the assessment tasks and the scoring scales. A valid assessment is an assessment that measures student performance of the stated curriculum and the taught curriculum—and nothing else. The examples in Appendix A illustrate a tight alignment between what is assessed and the stated curriculum (the standards-based content and skills outlined in the scoring scales). Notice that the scale for the Expressions learning goal (see p. 142) specifies at the Basic level that students need to be able to evaluate and simplify expressions and that the assessment tasks at the beginning of the test ask students to evaluate and simplify. Likewise, a descriptor for Level 4 (Advanced) of the same learning goal specifies that students need to create a real-life situation . . . , and the first assessment task for Level 4 asks them to do just that.

Similarly, to earn a score of 3 (Proficient) on the birth defects measurement topic, the scale specifies that students must analyze consequences of undergoing counseling or testing, and a Level 3 task on the assessment directs them to do that. (Note that this assessment is just one part of the assessment "package" developed for this topic. Other assessment tasks address other performances described in the scoring scale.) The same degree of stated curriculum-assessed curriculum alignment is found throughout both examples.

Most of us have experienced the frustration of preparing for what we thought was going to be on an exam and then finding out that the exam demanded something quite different. In the system advanced here, scoring scales—which are derived from essential elements of prioritized standards—drive both what is taught and what is assessed, thus promoting curricular alignment, assessment validity, and increased student learning.

The organization of the summative assessment. Educators exploring Destination 2 sometimes express initial confusion about how assessments—be they traditional paper-and-pencil exams, demonstrations, labs, projects, or other assessment types—are organized. The examples in Appendix A are of the more standard paper-and-pencil variety, but the organization shown there can be applied to other types of assessment tasks as well.

It is recommended that major assessments be organized by measurement topic and performance level. So in a unit of instruction consisting of three measurement topics, Levels 2, 3, and 4 for the first topic would be presented first, followed by Levels 2, 3, and 4 for the second measurement topic, and so on.

Organizing assessments in this manner facilitates the scoring process for teachers. If the student commits no major errors or omissions on the Level 2 assessment tasks for the first measurement topic, the student has earned a 2 (Basic). The teacher then goes on to evaluate the student's responses to the Level 3 tasks for that same topic. If the student commits no major errors or omissions on these tasks, the student has earned a 3 (Proficient). If, however, the student makes major errors or omissions at this level (sometimes a teacher judgment call), the student's score would be 2. Some scales employ half-point scores to allow for cases in which students get all of one level correct but only some correct at the next level. In these cases, the score would be a 2.5. If the student succeeds at Level 3, the teacher goes on to evaluate responses to Level 4 (Advanced) tasks. The teacher then repeats the whole process for the remaining two measurement topics.

Some teachers approach the assessment scoring process from the other direction by scoring the Advanced responses first. The logic is that if the student nails the Level 4 assessment tasks, there is no need to evaluate his or her Level 2 and 3 responses. However, this approach is recommended only if the Level 4 assessment tasks are comprehensive, and there is no chance that a student could do well on the Level 4 tasks without a command of the content and skills outlined in Levels 2 and 3 of the scoring scale.

The number and type of scores (total points, number correct, percentage, 0–4 scale, other) a student will be given on this summative exam. How many marks or scores will appear at the top of each student's exam, and what will be the nature of those marks, in the case of the algebra unit? For the birth defects unit?

In the case of the algebra unit test, students will receive two marks, ranging from 0 to 4—one for each learning goal (measurement topic). Students will receive only one mark for the birth defects assessment, again ranging from 0 to 4. No percentages or number correct out of number possible are recorded, as they are not only irrelevant but also counterproductive.

The number of correct responses is irrelevant in that often, more questions or tasks are needed to cover content at the Basic level because the performances at that level consist of smaller chunks of knowledge or skills (for example, vocabulary terms) than is the case for more comprehensive tasks at the Proficient and Advanced levels. Thus, assessing performance according to the number of items answered correctly can be very misleading.

Percentages are also misleading. Ninety-four percent of what—all DOK Level 1 tasks? I can make a 94 so easy that everyone gets it or so difficult that no one does. Your 75 may represent a higher level of performance than my 85. Scale scores based on specific content, skills, and performance expectations are much more informative and much more likely to be applied consistently across teachers than are either points or percentages.

The following are some more specific ways in which scale scores are superior to points or percentages in evaluating student work (I discuss these further in Chapter 11):

- Scale scores facilitate the formative assessment and improvement process.

- Scale scores lend themselves more directly to student self-evaluation and monitoring progress.

- Percentages and points focus student attention on collecting points and grades rather than on learning.

- Percentages and points "feel" like comparisons or competition with other students in the class.

- Scale scoring uses a language that facilitates a common understanding.

- Scale scoring facilitates differentiated instruction.

- Percentages and points don't identify proficiency or DOK levels; for example, 75 percent on an assessment that consists mostly of Level 3 and 4 tasks might reflect higher achievement than 100 percent on an assessment that is mostly Level 2.

- Percentages and points don't distinguish among students with the same or similar scores. For example, two students could both earn 60 percent on the same test but have very different performances—student A by answering four weighted Level 3 and 4 questions correctly and missing all 20 Level 2 questions, and student B by correctly answering all Level 2 questions and missing all Level 3 and 4 questions.

I hope this chapter's analysis and discussion in conjunction with the examples in Appendix A provide a concrete mental image of what instruction and assessment look like at Destination 2. Deft leadership and strategic support are needed to turn that image into reality, topics that we turn to in Chapter 11.

Leadership and Support to Sustain the Transition to Standards-Based Grading

In their guide to standards-based grading, Heflebower and colleagues (2014) relay the following reflection from someone presumably involved in leading the transition:

> This is not a task for the faint of heart.... All reform on a districtwide scale is tough, but moving a system to true standards-based grading is extraordinarily tough, long-term work and requires district leadership to tenaciously do the right thing for students. Waging war against the status quo requires the willingness to tackle layer after layer of difficulties in order to lead the way to new and purposeful assessment and grading practice. (p. 87)

The statement aptly describes the experiences of others who have challenged the classroom assessment and grading status quo.

Those on the front lines—teachers, counselors, administrators—both need and deserve in-depth, ongoing training and support before and during implementation of a comprehensive system of standards-based grading. A short list of the categories of training and support that district and school leadership teams must be prepared to provide when contemplating the adoption of systemic standards-based grading would include the following:

- **Standards-based education (SBE) training** to provide a thorough grounding in SBE, its components, and purposes.

- **Time** to collaboratively develop measurement topics, scoring scales, and leveled assessments.

- **Technical assistance** for creating strong, descriptive scoring scales; writing valid, reliable, and rigorous assessment tasks; and using SBE software.

- **SBE-compatible software** to assist with such matters as 0–4 scales, trend scoring, formative and summative assessment, and reports to parents.

- **Outreach assistance,** including talking points targeted at students and parents, and FAQs.

- **Input,** including opportunities to evaluate effectiveness and suggest modifications.

- **Individualized handholding and accountability** to reinforce the idea that what gets talked about, supported, and monitored gets implemented.

The following sections cover each of these categories in greater depth.

Standards-Based Education Training

Previous chapters of this book identified a number of practices, beliefs, characteristics, and strategies—about both traditional and standards-based grading—that those who are responsible for implementation must thoroughly explore and understand if standards-based education is to have any chance of succeeding as designed. Implementation with fidelity to design is critical to sustainability.

In addition, the purpose of the school's or district's standards-based grading initiative must be clear and well understood by all community stakeholders. Developing the knowledge base necessary for the rollout and implementation of an effective standards-based grading initiative takes time, money, leadership, and resolve. Research strongly supports the conclusion that ongoing modeling and mentoring are important elements in professional development that have an effect on student achievement. After examining several studies of professional development efforts, researchers concluded that a minimum of 30 hours of training is necessary in order for professional development work to have a positive and significant effect on student achievement (Yoon, Duncan, Lee, Scarloss, & Shapley, 2007). Obviously, then, the still prevalent one-shot workshop model is inadequate to the challenge of developing and implementing standards-based grading as envisioned in this book.

Time

In addition to time for professional development, time is essential for another purpose. As stated earlier in this book, to expect teams of teachers and support personnel to develop and implement a comprehensive system of standards-based education during weekly PLC meetings is to expect what has never happened and will never happen. Unpacking and prioritizing standards and creating measurement topics, scoring scales, and leveled assessment tasks requires big chunks of dedicated time.

Where can schools and districts find such time? Released time during the school day—either paid or by hiring substitute teachers to take over classrooms, summer paid work, and delayed starts are among the ways schools and districts develop standards-based education products without overburdening teachers. Another possibility is hiring recently retired teachers to do some of the writing.

At the high school where I served as principal for many years, we employed several of these methods to buy time for program development work. Most years, I was able to scrape together money from supplementary sources (vending machine profits, grants, rental income, budget savings) to pay volunteers a small stipend of $100 per day to work for a week during the summer. Unburdened by the demands of teaching, these teams were able to get a lot done during a relatively short period of time. During the school year, we occasionally hired substitute teachers to free up development teams for a day.

One of the most creative ways to buy time for program development work came to me one year from the school's science teachers. During the second semester of that year, we were a little overstaffed in the science department. By slightly increasing class sizes, we were able to reduce the number of class sections and free up one teacher full-time to write curriculum for a new integrated science course to be implemented the following year. What a gift!

Budgets are tighter than ever, but I continue to be impressed by the creative ways school administrators and teachers find time for program development work. Time to do the work necessary to create a guaranteed and viable curriculum is perhaps the most important support that school leaders can lend to the transition to standards-based grading.

Technical Assistance

Creating descriptive scoring scales around identified measurement topics and writing valid and reliable assessment tasks at the levels of rigor called for by those scales are two production tasks with which most practicing teachers will need technical assistance. In most schools and districts, neither the preservice training nor the inservice experiences of teachers is adequate to the task of developing these critical materials.

Larger districts sometimes have specialists who can provide this type of technical assistance to teams of teachers. Those that do not will need to hire outside consultants on a contract basis to provide these services.

SBE-Compatible Software

Technical problems have poisoned the standards-based education well in many pioneering schools and districts across the United States. Although almost all student information management systems now have standards-based grading options, the grade book features of some systems are not sufficiently aligned with the design of the grading system developed onsite to enable teacher-friendly data entry and data management. Software companies are not always able to make changes to their products to accommodate local demands because their software is used by multiple clients. Teachers are then frustrated by having to carry out time-consuming workaround procedures that add unnecessarily to the already considerable stress related to implementing a new initiative.

Districts may not be in the position to change student information management systems to accommodate new grading systems. The implementation plan outlined in Chapter 13 suggests investigating software-compatibility issues fairly early in the development process. In some cases, the implementation of a new grading system may need to be put on hold until the next software-purchasing cycle.

Outreach Assistance

District employees, and particularly teachers, experience discomfort and even resentment when they are unable to answer questions from students and parents about the proposed new system of grading. School and district employees must be well informed about the purpose or purposes of the initiative. In addition, responses to anticipated questions can be generated and even "practiced" using role-playing activities, with the full understanding that these group-generated responses are intended as optional tools for teachers. School personnel are free to respond in any way they feel appropriate—as long as they abide by the First Amendment.

Teachers may find it helpful to be prepared with an "elevator speech" to respond to parents and others who may confront them at the grocery store or in other nonschool settings with questions along the lines of

"What's going on at the school with that grading thing?" Heflebower and colleagues (2014) provide an example of a response:

> As you may know, the role of our staff is to educate all students to proficient levels. In order to do so, we are revising our grading practices to be aligned to the standards students must meet. That way, grades will be a clearer indication of what students have learned, not simply a measure of how much work they can turn in or how hard they might try in class. Learning is the indicator of success. (p. 95)

Similarly, Vatterott (2015) provides examples of letters to parents that explain what standards-based grading is and that offer answers to frequently asked questions.

The project communication plan (discussed in more detail in Chapter 13) should also serve as a useful tool for school personnel when they are confronted with questions or concerns from the public. Familiarization with what is available on the school or district website allows teachers and others to sometimes respond by directing the inquirer to the proper location on the website for answers to their questions.

Someone (preferably someone on the faculty or staff) needs to be available on short notice to answer teachers' questions and engage in collaborative problem solving. This person (or these people) must thoroughly understand the technical aspects of standards-based grading and have excellent communication and problem-solving skills. If the school, the district, or a nearby education services agency lacks this capacity, contracted services from an outside consultant should be explored.

Responses to frequently asked questions (FAQs) and to questions from individual teachers are among the outreach-assistance services a dedicated local or contracted resource person can provide. The following sections present replies that I developed in response to questions about standards-based grading from the faculty at James Campbell High School in Hawaii, as well as a response to an e-mail from an individual teacher at that same school. These responses are tied to specific policies developed over several years at Campbell and would not apply to all schools engaged in the transition to standards-based grading in every detail. That said, the important question is, Who in your school or district is prepared to play the role of personalized problem solver?

FAQs Regarding Standards-Based Grading at Campbell

1. How come teachers at Campbell aren't allowed to count homework and other formative assessments for more than 20 percent of students' session grades? The answer lies in the meaning and purpose of formative assessment. Formative assessment is, by definition, assessment for learning, not assessment of learning. The purpose of formative assessment is to find out where further work is needed before the administration of summative assessments. Students should not be penalized for making mistakes during the learning process.

The 80–20 rule at Campbell is a compromise between standards-based grading theory (formative assessments should not count as any part of students' grades) and teachers who believe students won't take formative assessment tasks seriously unless those tasks are given some weight in determining grades. Campbell data teams are encouraged to move toward grades based totally on summative assessment results.

2. What are the reasons for insisting all assessment tasks be scored using the 0–4 scale? What's wrong with just using percentages or total points? There are several reasons. The 0–4 scoring scale is tied directly to descriptive language on proficiency rubrics and therefore facilitates the formative assessment and improvement process. Students and teachers can look at the corresponding proficiency rubric and see exactly what a student who receives, for example, a 2 on an assessment needs to work on to move to a 3. Points and percentages are not as clear regarding what content and skills need to be the focus of future learning. For example, a 78 percent tells a student little about the specific content and skill that need further work.

The percentages/points approach focuses student attention on collecting points and grades ("How can I get more points?") rather than on learning ("What do I need to learn/do?").

Scoring using percentages/points "feels" like comparisons/competition with other students in the class ("What did you get?"). With rubric scoring it's all about you and the rubric.

Rubric scoring uses a language that facilitates a common understanding across campus for students; for example, a 3 is "proficient" in all classes.

Rubric scoring facilitates differentiated instruction—group all students trying to master Level 2 content and skills together, all Level 3 together, and so on.

Finally, percentages/points don't identify proficiency/DOK levels; for example, 75 percent on an assessment that is mostly Levels 3 and 4 might reflect higher achievement than a 100 percent on an assessment that is mostly Level 2.

3. If we are supposed to score and record assessment tasks on the 0–4 scale, why does our Jupiter grade book software still show percentages? Percentages were necessary during the transfer to Jupiter this fall as not all standards had been entered into the system. However, percentages are going away, hopefully by the start of the third quarter of this school year.

4. Can I add or deduct "points" to or from a student's session grade based on work ethic (behavior, incomplete assignments, class participation, tardiness, etc.)? The answer for most teachers is no. With standards-based grading, student grades are based only on those academic standards assigned to the course and not on work ethic and other behavioral issues. Grades at Campbell accurately reflect demonstrated performance on course academic standards, not a mixture of academic performance and behavior.

Work ethic behaviors are among standards in a few courses, specifically career and technical education (CTE) courses, in which case they can be included in student grades.

5. How is "extra credit" defined at Campbell, and why is it prohibited? Extra credit is defined as credit toward grades for work that lies outside course standards. Examples include "points" in a math class for contributing to the school's food drive or extra credit for neatness on a poster intended to demonstrate proficiency on a standard on cellular respiration in a biology class.

Extra credit should not be confused with reassessment. Giving students a second opportunity to demonstrate further learning is not extra credit, as the reassessment is based on the same course standard or standards as was the original assessment.

6. How many times must I offer students reassessment opportunities on summative assessments, and are there any conditions or limitations that apply? The bottom line is that students must be given more than one opportunity to demonstrate proficiency. The days of "teach, test, and move on" are gone. In many cases, one opportunity for reassessment may be all that time permits; in others, additional opportunities may be merited.

The purpose of providing reassessment opportunities is to encourage students to continue to work toward learning important content and skills, not to encourage "fishing expeditions." Therefore, students must produce evidence of additional learning (homework completed, computer tutorials, coming in for extra help, etc.) to earn a reassessment opportunity. Teachers can set reasonable restrictions as to when reassessment opportunities are offered.

7. With regard to reassessments, can I lower a student's grade for second attempts or enter an average of the two (or more) attempts as a final assessment grade? No. Work on a reassessment that meets the criteria identified for Level 4 performance is not a 3 because it was a second attempt. We want grades that accurately represent student competency at the conclusion of instruction. Demonstrating proficiency on Tuesday rather than Thursday isn't really important.

8. What about late work? Can I lower a student's grade for turning work in late? No, not if the work is turned in by the completion of the unit of study in which the work was assigned. The argument advanced in FAQ #7 applies here, too. Work that meets specific performance criteria does not become of inferior quality because of the date on which it was turned in. Lowering scores because of poor work habits (turning work in late) compromises the integrity of grades by mixing academic performance with work habits (see FAQ #4). Penalties for late work should be recorded under a work habit standard, not a course content or skill standard.

The underlying philosophy is that we want the work done, even if it's late (within reason), as our primary interest is in students learning the content or skills targeted by the assignment. In addition, the reasons students miss deadlines are sometimes due to conditions beyond their control and difficult or impossible for teachers to pass judgment on.

9. Should all formative assessments be entered into the grade book? No. Formative assessment results are intended to inform teaching and learning. As such, results of formal formative assessment should be evaluated and scored (0–4) but not necessarily graded. Most approaches to classroom formative assessment are informal (e.g., exit cards), and results need only a quick teacher evaluation regarding next steps.

10. Are all summative assessments to be common assessments? What about formative assessments? Campbell is working toward all summative assessments being common assessments to ensure consistency across data team teachers. However, as data teams are in different places regarding readiness, teachers are asked to use common summative assessments where available and add others as needed to enable valid and reliable conclusions regarding student proficiency.

The same is true for major formal formative assessments. (Formal formative assessments closely mirror future summative assessment structures and conditions, whereas informal formative assessments are short, quick checks for understanding often conducted orally.) The reason Campbell is moving toward some common formative assessments is that common data better enable data teams to do the work they were created to do: engage teachers of the same course in the collaborative analysis of student performance data and the improvement of instruction.

Of course, teachers will continue to supplement common formative assessments with regular formal and informal formative assessments of their own making.

11. How are DOK levels and our 0–4 rubric related, and what are the expectations regarding cognitive rigor in classroom instruction and assessment? One-to-one alignment is not possible as there are four DOK levels and only three actual proficiency levels (2–4) on the Campbell 0–4 scoring scale. In general, however, Level 2 on the Campbell scoring scale will most often call for DOK Levels 1 and 2 instructional and assessment tasks; Level 3, DOK Levels 2 and 3 tasks; and Level 4, DOK Levels 3 and 4 tasks.

12. Are we preparing kids for college? After all, formative assessment, reassessments, and rubric scoring are not what they're going to find in many of their college classes. As noted in Chapter 2, some colleges and universities are beginning to offer these features in their classes—for example, online practice quizzes (a type of formative assessment) that students can retake if they don't succeed on their first attempts (reassessment). Graduate students at the University of Hawaii report that they are able to submit their theses to their committees for suggested improvements before they turn in the final products (formative assessment). Law students can retake the bar exam until they pass (reassessment). Classroom assessment and grading practices are evolving even in higher education.

And even when assessment and grading practices at Campbell are *not* mirrored at the college and university level, college admissions officers and professors look for graduates who can read and understand complex texts, write well, think analytically and creatively, and demonstrate a command of discipline-specific foundational content and skills. Standards-based education can deliver such graduates. So although the specific grading practices may change, students will enter college with the college-ready knowledge and skills needed to be successful in a setting without formative assessments, reassessments, and rubric scoring.

Responses to an Individual Teacher's Questions in an E-mail

A teacher at James Campbell High School asked me the following two questions: (1) "How do I grade when half of Level 2s are wrong, some Level 3s are wrong, and one Level 4 is wrong?" (2) "I'm grading each question in each level for each of three standards covered on the exam. How do I come up with a final test score?"

Here is my response (which I titled "Assigning a Scoring Scale 0–4 Score to a Mixed Bag of Results"):

> Thanks for your questions. My response includes several levels of analyses, so here we go.
>
> 1. The first question to ask when students get some, but not all, items correct at Levels 2–4 is whether the items missed are tied directly to the targeted learning goal or a set of interdependent learning goals. Sometimes items are included in assessments that actually assess different (although related) content or skills, thus affecting assessment reliability. Items assessing content or skills not directly a part of the targeted learning goal(s) *as delineated in the corresponding scoring scale or scales* should be assessed separately.
>
> 2. Another question to ask is whether or not the errors represent *significant errors or omissions.* Minor errors that reflect carelessness, for example, rather than significant errors or omissions should be ignored.
>
> 3. Are the items properly classified (Levels 2–4) *from the student's perspective*? It is not uncommon to find that teachers have classified items at Levels 2 or 3 based on *their* understanding of the concept or skill only to find that upon reexamining the items from the students' perspective, the items ask for Level 3 or 4 performances.
>
> 4. Do all items at Levels 2 and 3 assess content or skills necessary to perform at Level 3 or 4? If not, why are they on the exam? *If* tight alignment exists among the progression of content and skill assessed in Levels 2–4, the performance shown on Level 4 is all that really matters.
>
> 5. Did formative assessment precede the summative? If not, there's your problem. If so, were these discrepancies noted

and addressed at those times? If all the criteria above are answered in the affirmative, I would ask this student to complete a series of reassessments, demonstrating Level 2 performance before being allowed to take the Level 3 items, and Level 3 performance before taking on Level 4 items. Yes, that takes time, but is the goal to get through the curriculum or to have students learn essential concepts and skills really well?

Now your second question. For SC.PS.7.Level 2, students can earn a 0–2 *for that entire section of the exam,* not a score on each item in that section. You have to decide if the student responses exhibit partial or full (2) understanding. If the score is a 0–1.5, then grading is over (assuming the criteria outlined under your first question are met). If the student's score on Level 2 merits a 2, then you continue to Level 3, and so on. The same applies to the other two standards addressed on the sample assessment you shared with me. On this exam, students will get three scores back, 0–4, one for each standard. They will not get a single combined score for the test.

Does this help?

You're doing good work here and asking the right questions. Keep it up!

Tim

Input

Everyone in the school community deserves periodic structured opportunities to share how the grading system is working and to offer suggestions for improvement. This is particularly true of teachers, as they experience the realities of implementation on a daily basis.

Teachers, as well as students and parents, are more comfortable taking a risk on something new if they know they will have opportunities to suggest modifications that promise to improve the system without compromising purpose. The project steering committee should be tasked with planning and conducting these formative assessment opportunities as well as with analyzing feedback and communicating resulting decisions and actions to stakeholders.

Individualized Handholding and Accountability

A school or district that decides to move toward standards-based education also needs to decide to make standards-based education a primary topic of teacher and administrator talk in school buildings for years to come. Too often the subject gets air time during the development and early implementation phases of the initiative, and then conversation— at faculty meetings, during evaluation conferences, between individual teachers and principals, in grade- or course-level meetings, during hiring interviews, and in budget and professional development discussions— turns to other emerging initiatives.

A few years ago I worked with a large urban school district in preparing teachers for a districtwide transition to standards-based grading. The district was led by talented and dedicated professionals at both the district and building levels, but for a variety of reasons, leadership for the standards-based grading initiative rested almost entirely on the shoulders of district personnel. Building principals were allowed to remain largely on the fringes. The result was that standards-based grading was not a topic of discussion at building faculty meetings, during professional learning community sessions, and in conversations between teachers and administrators. The initiative struggled to gain traction as teachers perceived that standards-based grading was not a top priority where they live—in their buildings.

Teachers need to hear on a regular basis that the proper implementation of standards-based grading remains at the top of their principal's to-do list. Teachers need to be asked how things are going and listened to when they bump into their principals in the hallway. Teachers need to see that standards-based grading and standards-based education receive priority attention in budgeting and professional development decisions. Teachers need to be held accountable for the proper implementation of standards-based grading through the supervision and evaluation process.

School principals play the major role in keeping the standards-based education ball rolling after initial implementation. As stated earlier in this chapter, what gets talked about, supported, and monitored gets implemented.

3

DESTINATION

Standards-Based Grading and Reporting

• • • • • • • • • • • • •

The first imperative of a successful transition to standards-based grading and reporting is to ensure that key players in the school community, starting with the district leadership team, thoroughly understand the characteristics that distinguish standards-based grading and reporting from more traditional grading practices: assessments are recorded by standard or measurement topic, not type; a 0–4 scale is used to evaluate assessments, not the number correct or percentages; students sometimes receive multiple scores on a single assessment; report cards display both topic scores and letter grades; and more. Each of these factors yields implications for day-to-day classroom instruction and assessment.

The devil's in the (planning) details. As with any other significant change initiative, the successful transition to standards-based grading is greatly facilitated by a well-thought-out, dynamic action plan. Where do we start? Is there a sequence of suggested steps we should consider when developing our action plan? What time frame should we be planning for? The answers to these and related questions lie in the development of a multiyear implementation plan, a leadership responsibility.

Experience teaches us that, without careful attention to process, moving to standards-based grading practices often results in pushback from students, parents, and even community members, and such pushback sometimes derails the initiative. Strategies for engaging the school community in the process of exploring best practices in classroom assessment and grading, and then taking action to close the gap between best practice and current practice, must be part of the planning process from the beginning.

Leadership challenges and opportunities include defining the roles and functions of parent groups and grading committees, confronting myths about standards-based grading, developing a project communication plan, learning from the experiences of pioneering school districts, and gaining the perspectives of and soliciting support from college admissions officers.

•   •   •   •   •   •   •   •   •   •   •   •   •   •

Standards-Based Versus Traditional Grading and Reporting Practices—and the Implications for Instruction and Assessment

Transitioning to standards-based grading and reporting involves much more than just changing grade books and report cards. As Heflebower and colleagues (2014) point out, "standards-based grading is a high-leverage strategy that has the power to improve every other element of the system" (p. 6). When the transition is done correctly, not only does grade recording and reporting change, but so do the clarity and presentation of course or subject expectations, the role of formative assessment, the approach taken to missing or late work, the opportunity for reassessment, the scale used to score work, the methods used to calculate final topic and course grades, and the degree to which students take ownership of learning. Whew!

To more clearly understand the implications, let's look at examples of a standards-based grade book and a standards-based report card. Beyond the differences in format compared with traditional approaches, these examples reveal the kinds of wide-ranging changes just enumerated.

A Sample Grade Book Page

Consider the grade book example from Robert Marzano (2006) in Figure 12.1. What can we learn about standards-based grading by looking at this example?

First, assessment scores are recorded by measurement topic (Probability, Data Analysis & Distributions, etc.), not by assessment type (tests, quizzes, homework, etc.). One implication of this standards-based grading characteristic is that teachers will need to be very clear about exactly which topic or standard a particular task assesses. A standards-based system has no place for tasks that are not tied directly to the topics or standards under study.

Second, assessment scores are in the form of scale scores and half scores from 0 through 4, not percentages, points, or letter grades. This method means that descriptive measurement scales outlining what students need to demonstrate at Levels 2 through 4 must be developed for each major measurement topic (e.g., Probability). Banks of measurement scales are available for adaptation and adoption, making this process a bit less challenging. (See Figure 9.5 for an example of a measurement scale.)

Third, the grade book example in Figure 12.1 shows that this district has chosen not to evaluate and record nonacademic (e.g., work ethic) topics. Evaluating and recording scores for nonacademic factors is an option but not a requirement of standards-based grading. Districts will have to decide whether or not they want to go down that path, and if so, whether or not nonacademic factors will be included in final course or subject grades.

Fourth, more than one measurement topic may be evaluated by the same assessment task. For example, we can see in Figure 12.1 that Probability was assessed (and taught, of course) along with Data Analysis & Distributions. Combining measurement topics on a single assessment occurs most often when skills are taught in the context of subject-matter content. In cases where a single assessment task is used to evaluate more than one topic or standard, teachers will need to be clear about which items evaluate which topics and at what level (2 through 4). Appendix A features two units of instruction that illustrate this topic/level/assessment alignment.

FIGURE 12.1
Measurement Topic View

Student: Jana

Assessment Key

1. Assignment Sept. 10	6. Assignment Sept. 24	11. Assignment Oct. 13
2. Test Sept. 13	7. Assignment Sept. 29	12. Test Oct. 15
3. Assignment Sept. 17	8. Test Oct. 2	13. Assignment Oct. 17
4. Test Sept. 20	9. Test Oct. 5	14. Final #1 Oct. 26
5. Test Sept. 22	10. Assignment Oct. 10	15. Final #2 Nov. 1

	Probability	Data Analysis & Distributions	Central Tendency & Dispersion	Measurement	Problem Solving	Patterns & Functions
1	.5	1.0				
2	1.5	.5				
3			2.0	1.0		
4	2.0	2.5				
5			1.5	1.0		
6					1.0	.5
7			3.0	2.0		
8	3.0	1.5				
9						1.5
10			2.5	2.0		
11					1.5	
12					2.0	
13						2.0
14	3.5	2.0			2.5	2.5
15			2.5	3.0	3.0	3.5
Final Score	3.65	1.71	2.49	2.41	2.80	3.65

Source: From *Classroom Assessment & Grading That Work* (p. 113), by Robert J. Marzano, 2006, Alexandria, VA: ASCD. Copyright 2006 by ASCD.

Fifth, assessment types are not weighted, per se, in arriving at a final topic score; for example, tests are not weighted differently from quizzes when entered into a standards-based grade book. This seems counterintuitive to many educators because tests usually cover more content than quizzes and should therefore be given more weight. In fact, in a standards-based system, more comprehensive assessments do have a greater effect on students' final unit and course grades than do quizzes or other limited-focus assessments, but in a way that is different from what most educators are accustomed to.

Longer, more comprehensive assessments—such as unit summative exams, projects, extended essays, and the like—usually assess multiple topics. Because they assess multiple topics, multiple scores are entered into the grade book, one for each topic assessed (see the answer to the second teacher e-mail question in Chapter 11 for an explanation of how assessment scoring works in this system). In contrast, shorter assessments, such as in-class activities and quizzes, may address only a single topic and therefore result in only one entry in the grade book. Thus, an assessment that generates multiple scores will have a greater "weight" than shorter assessments when calculating final grades. This shift in thinking is a difficult one for many teachers to make.

Sixth, final topic scores can be either trend scores or averages, whichever best fits the data. The rationale for trend scoring was explored in Chapter 4. In the case of the grade book page illustrated in Figure 12.1, the final score of 3.65 for the measurement topic Probability is clearly not the average of all scores recorded under that topic during the grading period. Instead, it is the final "power law" score, which takes into account the trajectory or trend of learning over the course of instruction.

A Sample Report Card

Continuing with the examination of artifacts that illuminate key features and characteristics of standards-based grading, let's look at the sample report card in Figure 12.2. What can we learn from this example?

FIGURE 12.2
Report Card with Grades and Topic Scores

Name:	Aida Haystead	**Subject Areas:**	
Address:	123 Some Street	Language Arts	B
City:	Anytown, CO 80000	Mathematics	B
Grade Level:	5	Science	D
Homeroom:	Ms. Becker	Social Studies	A
		Art	B

Language Arts

Reading:

Word Recognition and Vocabulary	3.5	
Reading for Main Idea	2.5	
Literary Analysis	3.0	

Writing:

Language Conventions	4.0	
Organization and Focus	2.0	
Research and Technology	1.5	
Evaluation and Revision	2.5	
Writing Applications	1.0	

Listening and Speaking:

Comprehension	3.0	
Organization and Delivery	3.5	
Analysis and Evaluation of Oral Media	2.0	
Speaking Applications	2.0	

Life Skills:

Participation	4.0	
Work Completion	3.0	
Behavior	4.0	
Working in Groups	2.5	

Mathematics

Number Systems	4.0	
Estimation	2.5	
Addition/Subtraction	3.5	
Multiplication/Division	3.5	
Ratio/Proportion/Percent	0.5	

Life Skills:

Participation	4.0	
Work Completion	2.5	
Behavior	3.0	
Working in Groups	2.0	

(Continues on next page)

FIGURE 12.2

Report Card with Grades and Topic Scores *(continued)*

Science		
Matter and Energy	1.5	
Forces of Nature	2.5	
Diversity of Life	1.0	
Human Identity	2.0	
Interdependence of Life	0.5	
Life Skills:		
Participation	1.5	
Work Completion	2.0	
Behavior	3.0	
Working in Groups	1.0	
Social Studies		
The Influence of Culture	3.0	
Current Events	3.5	
Personal Responsibility	4.0	
Government Representation	4.0	
Human and Civil Rights	3.0	
Life Skills:		
Participation	4.0	
Work Completion	4.0	
Behavior	4.0	
Working in Groups	3.5	
Art		
Purposes of Art	1.5	
Art Skills	2.5	
Art and Culture	3.0	
Life Skills:		
Participation	2.5	
Work Completion	2.0	
Behavior	4.0	
Working in Groups	3.0	

Source: From *What Works in Schools: Translating Research into Action* by Robert J. Marzano, 2003, pp. 41–42. Copyright 2003 by ASCD.

First, both final topic grades and overall course letter grades are reported. This does not have to be the case, as some schools and districts have chosen to report only final topic scores. I recommend a dual system of reporting student achievement at the secondary level, as parents at that level tend to be reluctant to give up traditional letter grades. A single letter grade based on multiple disparate topics is of questionable value—a point that has been addressed earlier in this book—but leaders sometimes have to decide which battles are worth fighting. Final topic scores can be combined to form a single course letter grade rather easily. Figure 12.3 shows three examples of simple conversion metrics.

Second, this report card gives the interested parent—as well as next year's teacher—much more information about the student's strengths and weaknesses than would a traditional report card with letter grades only. For example, a parent can see that in mathematics the student is strong in Number Systems but quite weak in her understanding of Ratio/Proportion/Percent. Next year's teacher should be interested in that information, too, as background information on the student's learning needs.

Third, this district has decided to report nonacademic factors (e.g., Participation), an option in standards-based grading, as previously discussed.

Fourth, a fair amount of detail is included in this example, particularly in the Language Arts section. Some schools and districts choose to include only major headings on the report card (Reading, Writing, Listening and Speaking) for the sake of simplicity while still keeping track of individual topic scores to facilitate monitoring progress, instructional planning, and student ownership of learning. Again, this is an individual district decision.

The Bigger Picture

So picture this. Course-alike, grade-level, or subject-area teams have gotten together to identify which standards or parts of standards students should master in each course or grade level. The teams have unpacked standards to identify essential elements, and they have developed scoring scales that describe leveled performance expectations for related sets

FIGURE 12.3

Converting Scale Scores to Letter Grades and Percentages

Converting Scale Scores to Letter Grades

3.00–4.00 = A	1.50–1.99 = D
2.50–2.99 = B	Below 1.50 = F
2.00–2.49 = C	

Converting Scale Scores to Letter Grades with Plus and Minus

3.75–4.00 = A+	2.17–2.33 = C
3.26–3.74 = A	2.00–2.16 = C–
3.00–3.25 = A–	1.76–1.99 = D+
2.84–2.99 = B+	1.26–1.75 = D
2.67–2.83 = B	1.00–1.25 = D–
2.50–2.66 = B–	< 1.00 = F
2.34–2.49 = C+	

Converting Scale Scores to Letter Grades and Percentage Points

	3.90–4.00 = 100
	3.80–3.89 = 99
	3.70–3.79 = 98
	3.60–3.69 = 97
	3.50–3.59 = 96
3.00–4.00 = A	3.40–3.49 = 95
	3.30–3.39 = 94
	3.20–3.29 = 93
	3.10–3.19 = 92
	3.00–3.09 = 91

of essential elements. Teachers have developed or revised instructional units that encompass measurement topics that fit together instruction-ally, given the school or district's chosen curriculum, and formative and summative assessments have been devised to assess each level of each measurement topic.

Students are taught to monitor and track their performance, and are given chances for reassessment, as necessary, upon demonstration of further learning. Teachers calculate final topic scores using either trend scores or averaging, depending on which method best fits the data, and they report student achievement using just topic scores in elementary schools and both topic scores and composite letter grades in secondary schools.

The implications of these developments for day-to-day classroom instruction and assessment are monumental, transformational, and exciting.

Developing a Multiyear Transition and Implementation Plan

It probably does not take much convincing for people to agree that an initiative as complex and transformational as the transition to standards-based grading and related changes in teaching and learning needs a plan. Figure 13.1 identifies actions that might be taken over a four-year transition and implementation period.

The specifics of a district transition and implementation plan may differ in several respects. For example, there is nothing magical about a time span of four years. Existing initiatives, available resources, internal capacity, organization conditions (covered in Chapter 8), and prior learning and preparation may suggest the wisdom of a three-year or a five-year plan. However, one year is definitely not enough time to transition to standards-based grading, even under the most favorable conditions, and a two-year plan would be very tight.

In addition, both the specifics steps and their placement on the time line will vary from district to district depending on influencing factors such as those just listed. An implementation plan must be tailored to meet local contexts and conditions and open to frequent revision as circumstances dictate.

FIGURE 13.1
Four-Year Plan for Transitioning to Standards-Based Grading

Year 1: Inquiry and Communication

- Review the research on best practices.
- Establish a leadership committee on grading practices.
- Conduct focus group sessions on school/district grading practices, including teachers, students, and parents.
- Conduct a gap analysis—best practice versus current practice.
- Build a rationale/moral purpose for change.
- Determine the need for outside consultants and other resources.

Year 2: Capacity Building

- Educate teachers and administrators on the tenets of standards-based education (SBE).
- Provide professional development on necessary prerequisite knowledge.
- Provide time and tech support for teams of teachers to develop learning goals, scoring scales, and leveled assessments for a unit of instruction. *Teach the unit.*
- Equip teachers and administrators to explain the initiative and its purposes and to answer FAQs.
- Educate students, parents, and BOE members about grading issues, best practices, and SBE.
- Begin exploration of report card formats.

Year 3: Development

- Continue developing SBE units of instruction.
- Align instructional materials.
- Develop core beliefs.
- Develop a school/district grading policy.
- Explore/create SBE-grading software alignment.
- Determine project evaluation criteria and processes.
- Adapt/adopt/pilot standards-based grading (SBG) report card.
- Continue student, parent, and BOE education.
- Continue implementation of communication plan.

(Continues on next page)

FIGURE 13.1

**Four-Year Plan for Transitioning
to Standards-Based Grading** *(continued)*

Year 4: Implementation

- Continue ongoing training of new teachers.
- Carry out project's formative assessment activities.
- Continue implementation of communication plan.
- Monitor implementation and provide ongoing support, modeling, and coaching.

The following sections review the components of the sample plan in Figure 13.1. The intent is to deepen understanding of the work to be undertaken, keeping in mind the importance of customizing the plan to address specific local needs and conditions.

Year 1: Inquiry and Communication

Year 1 gets the ball rolling with inquiry into the gap between current practice and best practice and communicating the purpose, process, and products of the initiative to interested stakeholders.

One of the first things to do is to establish a steering committee on grading practices that is tasked with the responsibility of charting the direction and coordinating the work of the project. Among the committee's responsibilities are those of approving, monitoring, and modifying the transition and implementation plan.

Care should be taken to ensure the committee is representative of all major stakeholders in the community, although not necessarily in equal numbers. Teachers possess topic expertise and will be on the front lines of carrying out whatever comes out of the initiative. That being the case, teachers should be represented in larger numbers than other stakeholder groups on the committee. An application process for committee membership should be established that is transparent and open to everyone in the community. Individuals who possess special expertise or who are particularly influential among stakeholder groups, including those who harbor initial reservations about the direction the project might take, should be encouraged to apply.

Tasks for the committee's first meeting include the selection of cochairs, the clarification of the committee's charge and authority (decision making or advisory), the development of working norms, and the establishment of meeting dates and times.

The grading practices steering committee must become well versed in classroom assessment and best-practices research as it relates to grading. This is one place in the process where outside expertise may be needed. Using that research as a basis, the committee should establish processes to ascertain current perceptions, practices, and beliefs of teachers, administrators, students, and parents so that a gap analysis of current practices versus best practices can be conducted.

There are many different approaches a school or district might take to assess the alignment of current practice and best practice or to ascertain perceptions about grading practices from key stakeholder groups. For example, O'Connor's 15 fixes (2010), a research-based list of classroom assessment and grading best practices, could be adapted as a survey instrument with a scale (from strongly disagree to strongly agree) and administered to teachers to determine current practices. Results would inform steering committee members about the areas on which future professional development should focus.

The "Have you ever . . ." questions in Chapter 14 (pp. 123–124) could be used in a survey or focus group format to find out how parents feel about current grading practices and how ready they are to explore changes. Modifications of those questions can be easily made to fit other stakeholder groups, such as students. Data from these queries would direct future planning and action by the steering committee and other school and district leaders.

Again, many different formats can be used to collect gap analysis data. Formats from information-gathering tools on other topics can even be modified to fit the task at hand. What's important is that designers are clear about the purpose of the data to be collected and that the format chosen is conducive to the kind of information sought.

Another important first-year task is to establish and communicate the moral purpose for the initiative. Why are we looking at classroom assessment and grading practices? What are the potential benefits to students? Challenging the status quo just because standards-based grading is a hot topic among education groups will not provide the motivation necessary to sustain the initiative through the hard work and controversy sure to come.

Finally, a communication plan should be created early in the development process to communicate the purpose, process, and products of the work to all stakeholders. The development of a communication plan might best be delegated by the steering committee to an ad hoc working committee consisting of a few steering committee members and district personnel with expertise in this area. The goal of the communication plan is to avoid having anyone say, "Why weren't we told about . . . ?" (even though some will). Developing a communication plan is explored further in Chapter 14.

Year 2: Capacity Building

Year 2 of this sample transition and implementation plan focuses on educating students, parents, and board of education members on best practices for classroom assessment and grading and equipping teachers and administrators with the knowledge, skills, and experiences they need so they can deepen their understanding of standards-based grading.

Providing teams of teachers with time and technical support to develop a standards-based unit of instruction that they will actually pilot in their classrooms is the anchor activity of the Year 2 plan. There is no better way to get a firm grasp of a new way of doing something than to actually do it. These pilot teams will then be equipped to share what they learned from the experience with the steering committee and with their colleagues in the school. Given ongoing support and the fact that teachers volunteering to be in a pilot program are typically predisposed toward the success of the initiative, the pilot experience will likely be mostly positive and will thus help build momentum toward the transition. The Home Depot slogan "Let's do this" is apropos.

Creating a standards-based unit of instruction includes developing measurement topics, scoring scales, and matching leveled assessments. Pilot teachers will need to be trained on the processes they are to use to develop these standards-based components before actually beginning their development work (see Chapters 9 and 10). Year 2 is also a good time to begin familiarizing all teachers and administrators with the tenets of standards-based grading, focusing on counterproductive practices and the distinguishing characteristics of standards-based grading as outlined in Chapters 1 through 7 and Chapter 12, respectively.

An alternative to the pilot teacher approach is to ask all grade-level or course-alike teams to develop and teach one standards-based unit of instruction. The advantage of this approach is that it gets everyone involved. Disadvantages include spreading technical support thin, the challenge of training everyone early on in the development process (either or both of which increase the possibility of creating poor-quality products), and the possibility that detractors might sabotage early efforts in an attempt to discredit the project.

Students, parents, and board of education members also need to be brought into the loop. Members of the steering committee might help inform others in their stakeholder groups, perhaps joined by members of pilot teacher teams. Bringing students, parents, and board of education members up to speed is another area where engaging the services of outside experts is often a good investment. The project communication plan (see Chapter 14) will also play a key role in keeping these groups informed.

Parents expect district leaders and employees to be knowledgeable about any change initiative that is going to have an effect on their children. As previously discussed, teachers in particular resent being put into the position of not being able to answer questions from parents about standards-based grading and the attendant changes to classroom instruction and assessment. In addition to sharing the rationale for and purpose of the standards-based grading initiative with all faculty and staff, the steering committee should consider developing a list of frequently asked questions and responses (see examples in Chapter 11). This list should be shared with board members as well. Time might be set aside at the building level to role-play likely parent-teacher interactions to help teachers gain confidence in their ability to respond in an informed manner.

Finally, Year 2 is a good time for the steering committee to begin exploring standards-based report card formats. Examples from schools and districts around the country are readily available for comparison, and it will take time to get input from all stakeholder groups before deciding on a format.

Year 3: Development

Year 3 is a time for bringing all the components under development in Years 1 and 2 to fruition and gathering them together. Teams of teachers will continue to convert existing units to standards-based units and create new units as needed, capitalizing on what was learned in initial efforts during Year 2. They will align instructional materials with units of instruction, as described in Chapter 9.

By this point in the process, enough learning and dialogue have occurred to build consensus around a school or district grading policy, led by the steering committee. Core beliefs based on best-practices research and shaped by local community values and expectations are spelled out early in the policy. Project evaluation criteria and processes are developed to ensure that standards-based grading is achieving the intended purpose or purposes of the initiative and are used primarily for the purpose of formative assessment.

Project evaluation criteria should be tied directly to the intended outcome or outcomes of the initiative as identified in Year 1 (build a rationale/moral purpose for change). If one of the purposes for making changes to classroom assessment and grading practices is to better align instruction and assessment with college readiness expectations, then data on college acceptance, remediation, and graduation rates as well as related anecdotal data and testimonials should be collected and analyzed. If the change rationale includes the intent to make performance expectations consistent across teachers of the same course or grade level, then comparative data from common assessments, grade distributions, and rates of interreliability agreement could be among the evaluation criteria. If an intended outcome of the initiative is to increase student achievement, then baseline and ongoing achievement data (including test scores, graduation rates, grade point averages, scholarships awarded, and college credits and certificates earned) should be collected and analyzed. Teachers could be surveyed periodically to get their perceptions on how well students come to them prepared for success.

Several years ago, I heard someone describe the kind of program evaluation that typically occurs in education as "cardiac assessment—I don't have any data, but I know in my heart that this program is good for kids." We can and must do better than that, which is why identifying program evaluation criteria belongs in a classroom assessment and grading transition and implementation plan.

Year 3 is also the year to move to closure on a new report card format, to make whatever adjustments to district grading software are necessary to ensure consistency with new grading practices and policies, and to make the process of recording and reporting student achievement as teacher-friendly as possible. Software training for teachers will likely be a part of these action steps.

Throughout the entire development process, and certainly during Year 3 of the transition and implementation plan, ongoing education of and communication with students, parents, and board members is critical to the sustainability of the initiative.

Year 4: Implementation

And now, the moment we have all been waiting for—implementation.

During the first couple of years of implementation and periodically thereafter, formative assessment of the project's effectiveness in fulfilling its purpose or purposes; student, parent, and teacher satisfaction; and, most important, the effect of standards-based grading on student achievement must be planned for and conducted. Implementation must be monitored for fidelity across teachers and schools, and time and resources must be provided to make adjustments called for as indicated by formative assessment data. Teachers will continue to benefit from modeling of standards-based strategies by teacher leaders and administrators. All stakeholders deserve and expect to be kept informed of progress, problems, and modifications.

Too often schools and districts abandon the focus on standards-based grading after implementation, expecting teachers to "just run with it." New teachers receive scant training upon entering the organization, and veteran teachers lack ongoing support and monitoring. Teachers are further distracted by the introduction of "the next new thing" by school or district leaders in spite of what research and common sense tell us about the time it takes to master a new set of skills or practices. Deterioration begins, slowly but surely.

Failure to give due diligence to the activities of Year 4 (and beyond) all but guarantees disappointing results in years to come. The qualifier attached to the interpretation of the transition and implementation plan outlined in Figure 13.1 at the beginning of this chapter bears repeating— the specifics of a school or district plan may differ in several respects due to any number of local circumstances and conditions. What is also a certainty is that failing to plan is the same as planning to fail.

Community Engagement and Communication

Community engagement and involvement are obviously important to the success and sustainability of a standards-based grading initiative. The literature on the topic is filled with stories of schools and districts that got out ahead of their communities and suffered setbacks or were forced to abandon the project altogether as a result. Both the overall project transition and implementation plan (see Chapter 13) and its communication component should be clear about which stakeholders will be involved in the exploration and development of standards-based grading and how they will be involved.

A communication plan must *proactively answer people's questions and concerns* with *clear and consistent* messages *delivered through a variety of communication channels.* To act on the key phrases (in italics) in this description of the characteristics of an effective communication plan, it is helpful to revisit the distinction between *messaging* and *connecting*.

Messaging and Connecting: What's the Difference?

Messaging is all about informing. Well-thought-out messaging can be useful in conveying specific types of new information, countering misperceptions, addressing gaps in knowledge among the broader school community, and putting ideas on the table for further discussion. As with all communication, messaging is most effective when it avoids insider jargon and shop talk and uses language and examples that are human, compelling, and concrete.

Connecting is about dialogue—listening and understanding rather than advocating and persuading. It is not a debate. Instead, participants are looking for common ground, and district leaders are asking members of the school community to join them in problem solving (e.g., addressing counterproductive classroom assessment and grading practices).

Both messaging and connecting serve important purposes when implementing standards-based grading. The key to effective communication is a balanced approach and knowing when to employ each type of communication.

When the goal is public engagement, recommended ground rules include the following:

- Take a big-tent approach. Include all stakeholders (diverse constituencies) from the beginning and develop genuine relationships.

- Be sure to talk and listen.

- Sing from the same songbook. Focus on internal communications and consider everyone a messenger—that is, make sure everyone is knowledgeable and able to explain the rationale behind standards-based grading. In this regard, consider the following:

    ▷ The most important messengers are those closest to the kids and families.

    ▷ Develop specific talking points for teachers and principals.

    ▷ Publish a statement spelling out the district's beliefs about classroom assessment and grading.

- Use existing communications methods and structures, such as the PTA.

- Ensure that you use simple, clear, consistent messages for all and differentiate for key audiences.

- Methods matter. Communication tools and delivery mechanisms are important. Lectures and other one-way communications extolling the virtues of new grading practices have limited effectiveness and may even breed defensiveness or be counterproductive. Home coffees and other two-way opportunities for genuine dialogue are more likely to result in an atmosphere of collaborative problem solving. Keep in mind, too, that printed newsletters sent home with students seldom reach their intended audiences, particularly at the secondary level; social media is where it's at in the 21st century.

- A good defense is a better offense. Start communicating now!

- Be proactive rather than reactive. Educate the school community on the truths of standards-based grading. Let them know how hard this effort is—risks, costs, trade-offs.

- Provide community members with resources on standards-based grading. A sample of such resources follows:

  ▷ "Starting the Conversation About Grading" by Susan M. Brookhart (2011). In *Educational Leadership, 69*(3), 10–14. Available: http://www.ascd.org/publications/educational-leadership/nov11/vol69/num03/Starting-the-Conversation-About-Grading.aspx

  ▷ *Are Zeros Fair? An Analysis of Grading Practices* by James Cristea (2007, June). Cabrini College. Available: http://sciencefool.com/cabrini/AreZerosFair.pdf

  ▷ "Grading Practices: The Third Rail" by Jeffrey A. Erickson (2010). In *Principal Leadership, 10*(7), 22–24.

  ▷ "Grade Inflation: Killing with Kindness?" by Bryan Goodwin (2011). In *Educational Leadership, 69*(3), 80–81. Available: http://www.ascd.org/publications/educational-leadership/nov11/vol69/num03/Grade-Inflation@-Killing-with-Kindness%C2%A2.aspx

▷ "Five Obstacles to Grading Reform" by Thomas R. Guskey (2011). In *Educational Leadership, 69*(1), 16–21. Available: http://www.ascd.org/publications/educational-leadership/nov11/vol69/num03/Five-Obstacles-to-Grading-Reform.aspx

▷ "Grading Policies That Work Against Standards . . . and How to Fix Them" by Thomas R. Guskey (2000). *NASSP Bulletin, 84*(620), 20–29. Available: http://www.hsd.k12.or.us/Portals/0/district/Grading%20Reporting/Grading/Guskey%202000%20Grading%20policies%20that%20work%20against%20standards.pdf

▷ "Zero Alternatives" by Thomas R. Guskey (2004). *Principal Leadership, 5*(2), 49–53. Available: http://www.schoolschedulingassociates.com/wp-content/uploads/canady/zero.pdf

▷ "Finding Your Grading Compass" by Carol Ann Tomlinson (2011). *Educational Leadership, 69*(3), 86–87. Available: http://www.ascd.org/publications/educational-leadership/nov11/vol69/num03/Finding-Your-Grading-Compass.aspx

▷ "Best Practices in Grading" by School District of Waukesha (Wisconsin) (2007). Available: http://waukesha.k12.wi.us/Portals/0/cgarcia/gradingbestpracticesver2sep09.pdf

Finally, conducting community meetings that enlighten rather than polarize and knowing how to overcome initial resistance are important skill sets for those leading the transition to standards-based grading. When planning a community meeting intended to engage school community members, it is helpful to ask the following three questions:

• How much time will be devoted to presenting versus hearing what people have to say? Something in the neighborhood of a 1:2 ratio is a good target—that is, spend twice as much time listening as talking.

• How will you respond when people disagree with you?

• What will you do after the meeting? Major findings and lessons learned should be identified and follow-up action steps developed and assigned within a couple of weeks of the meeting. This is good work for the project steering committee. A summary of the above should be made available to stakeholders using a variety of media.

Thinking through these questions during the planning process can increase the odds that the meeting will result in enlightenment rather than polarization.

Going for the heart, not the brain; telling stories; and putting a human face on standards-based grading can help reduce initial resistance. Listen to complaints and attempt to identify underlying issues. Build on strengths.

An effective approach to engaging communities before resistance builds is to invite them to tell their own stories. Here are some questions you can use to jump-start a discussion with parents, for example, on why standards-based grading makes sense:

Have you ever . . .

• Been unclear about what in a lesson or unit was important and what was supplemental or just nice to know?

• Thought you knew what the teacher or professor wanted, and prepared for the test accordingly, only to find out that the test was on something completely different?

• Wished you or your child had had more opportunities along the way to test understanding before the big test?

• Had the feeling that your grade or your son's or daughter's grade in a course could be significantly different depending on to which teacher/ professor you or your child was assigned?

• Felt that what you or your son or daughter would learn in a class could vary significantly depending upon which teacher/professor you or your child was assigned to?

• Wished you had a second chance to demonstrate your knowledge, having learned from your mistakes on the first assessment?

• Felt that you or your child were not challenged to think at cognitively demanding levels in a class or course?

- Been either bored or "lost," or felt your child was bored or lost, because instruction delivered to the entire class did not fit where you or your child were at the time?

- Felt that grades did not necessarily reflect course knowledge and skills but rather a combination of course knowledge and skills and teacher-pleasing behaviors, such as homework completion, tardiness, extra credit, and pleasant demeanor?

Audience, Medium, and Message: Key Elements of a Communication Plan

Communication specialists know the importance of being clear about *audience, medium,* and *message* when developing a communication plan.

With regard to the transition to standards-based grading, the audiences are, of course, the key stakeholder groups project leaders want to keep engaged, informed, and supportive. Obvious targets are teachers and other school employees, students, parents, and school board members. Perhaps less obvious but also important are local elected officials, real estate agents, business leaders, and higher education officials. Delineation of audience is a key component of an effective communication plan. Simple spreadsheets such as those displayed in Figures 14.1, 14.2, and 14.3 as part of an overall communication plan can help manage the communication process.

FIGURE 14.1
Grid for Planning Communication for Internal Audiences

Audiences: Internal	Message	Medium	Target Dates	Persons/ Positions Responsible

FIGURE 14.2

Grid for Planning Communication for External Audiences

Audiences: External	Message	Medium	Target Dates	Persons/ Positions Responsible

FIGURE 14.3

Grid for Planning Engagement Strategies for Stakeholder Groups

Stakeholder Group	Engagement Strategy	Target Dates	Persons/Positions Responsible

The *media* by which individuals, groups, and organizations communicate have changed dramatically over the last few years. If the only tool in your communication tool box is the monthly print newsletter, you are in trouble. And it is worth noting that different media appeal to different audiences. Defining and matching audience with medium is another distinguishing feature of an effective communication plan.

Figure 14.4 includes a partial list of potential communication tools. The intent is not to suggest that a district should be using all of these tools, but rather that it should use both one-way and two-way communication tools, depending on audience and message.

Vatterott (2015) offers a suggestion regarding messaging to parents regardless of the medium employed. She suggests beginning the

FIGURE 14.4

Tools for Messaging and Connecting

One-Way	Two-Way
• Newsletters	• Community forums
• Fliers	• Focus groups
• Back-to-school nights	• Home coffees
• Computer-generated calls	• Parent-teacher conferences
• E-mail blasts	• Phone calls
• Online postings	• E-mail
• URLs	• Facebook
	• Twitter
	• Hashtags
	• Crowdsourcing
	• Webinars
	• Blogs
	• Google Voice
	• Google Forms
	• Google Hangouts
	• District/school
	• Voxer

conversation with parents by focusing on school improvement rather than grading:

> The changes we propose for our students' learning
>
> • are research based,
>
> • are about improving student achievement, and
>
> • will better prepare our students for college and careers.
>
> As a result of our goals, it makes sense that we would change these things about grading. (p. 97)

In other words, changes in grading practices are a means to an end—improved student learning.

Vatterott goes so far as to suggest avoiding the term "standards-based grading" as that title connotes different things to different people and has generated negative alarmist publicity, albeit often inaccurate and unfounded. Vatterott offers some alternate possibilities for consideration: "grading for learning," "learner-focused learning," and "learner-centered assessment and reporting" (p. 97).

Top Ten List of Questions to Address

One often effective method of packaging the message is to present it in the form of responses to questions that define the project. In the style of recently retired television host David Letterman, the following are examples of questions—presented as a "Top Ten List" in reverse order—that will most likely need to be addressed in a communication plan, using a variety of formats and media—for standards-based grading.

Question Number 10: What are you trying to accomplish? Stakeholders, particularly parents and school board members, will expect school and district personnel to be clear about the intended outcome or outcomes of the initiative. Why standards-based grading? What current problems are we trying to solve?

Question Number 9: What will success look like? Closely related to Question Number 10, school and district communications must help members of the school community create a mental picture of what teaching and learning will look like if the initiative is successful—in my school, in my classroom, for my child, for me as a parent. Whether it is condominiums or standards-based grading, most people will not buy into something they cannot see, at least in their mind's eye.

Question Number 8: How will you track and measure success? This question is answered initially by showing constituents that Year 3 of the overall project transition and implementation plan (as described in Chapter 13) includes identification of project evaluation criteria and processes. During and after the writing of the evaluation criteria and processes, the steering committee should make drafts available to stakeholder groups.

The evaluation processes themselves should include input from interested stakeholders, along with information about how and when results will be shared.

Question Number 7: What research supports this change? Savvy constituents will be interested in seeing the research that supports the move to standards-based grading. And they will not just rely on what the school district provides—they will be on the Internet themselves, seeking information. Simply enter "research on standards-based grading" into your search engine, and a variety of reports, mostly credible, will be available for exploration.

The Internet is full of information and misinformation on standards-based grading—and most every other topic imaginable. Given that reality, school and district leaders will first need to educate the community on the difference between research and testimonials. (The issue of testimonials comes more into play with Question Number 6.)

A second recommended strategy is to include in what is provided to the community in response to this question research that explores findings related to positive effect, negative effect, and no effect on student learning. Doing so demonstrates a commitment to intellectual honesty and builds trust. In addition, much can be learned from adoptions that did not produce positive results.

The Raymond School District in Washington State has a page on its website titled "Research/Links for Standards-based Reporting" (http://www.raymondk12.org/component/content/article/143-standards-based-grading/192-researchlinks-for-standards-based-reporting). It provides an excellent example of how a school or district might answer the question "What research supports this change?"

Question Number 6: Who else is doing this, and has it been successful? Another version of this question is "Our kids aren't going to be used as guinea pigs, are they?" Parents and students have a legitimate interest in knowing that what is being proposed is not something that no one has ever done before. Relatively few schools have made the move to competency-based education as described in Chapter 15, and those that have tend to be smaller experimental or alternative schools of some type. But there are a number of schools—public and private; elementary and secondary; small and large; rural, suburban, and urban—that have successfully implemented and sustained standards-based grading systems.

Appendix B contains a partial list of more than 30 schools and districts reporting implementation of some form or some aspects of standards-based grading. These schools and districts vary considerably in the scope and nature of their implementation, with some reflecting all aspects of standards-based grading as described in Chapters 9 and 10 and others implementing just one or two.

Oregon now requires that student grades be based on academic achievement only and not on nonacademic factors like neatness, late work, or behavior. New grading policies developed in compliance with state law have been enacted in Portland, Beaverton, Hillsboro, Tigard-Tualatin, Lake Oswego, Reynolds, Forest Grove, and Sherwood.

Of course, one can probably find horror stories about standards-based grading or some aspect of it for each of these schools and districts. Here again, district and school leaders must help concerned community members distinguish between research and testimonials, evaluate sources, and learn from those implementations that did not go well.

Question Number 5: How does standards-based grading fit into the "big picture" in our district? The questions behind this question are these: Is standards-based grading part of a long-term comprehensive improvement plan for our school or district, or is it just the latest hot topic at education conferences? Does it enhance what we are already doing, or is it just one more thing to do?

Most districts already have some school improvement issues on their plate—differentiated instruction, value-added teacher evaluation, data-driven decision making, Common Core State Standards, the whole child movement, project-based learning, one-to-one technology initiatives, flipped classrooms, blended instruction—the list goes on. In addition to the risk of contributing to what Doug Reeves and others call "initiative fatigue," legitimate concerns arise as to "the fit" of standards-based grading with what has already been launched. In too many schools and districts, every year brings the introduction of new initiatives without an explanation as to how they collectively complement one another in the quest of a common goal.

How does standards-based education fit into our overall picture? How does it support other initiatives to which we have already devoted time, energy, and money? What is the overarching goal toward which all initiatives are directed? District leadership—administrators and teachers—must be able to answer these questions. One possible activity is to ask groups of teachers, for example, to construct an infographic, using both linguistic and nonlinguistic representations, that depict how everything fits together.

One year at a high school where I served as principal, we devoted an entire faculty meeting to this exercise to clarify how our improvement initiatives fit together. Teachers worked as department teams to construct infographics that, from their perspectives, represented the "big picture" of school improvement at the school. The administrative team participated as a group in the exercise as well.

The results were both interesting and informative. People gained clarity by seeing and hearing how others in the building pictured what was going on. We also learned where our gaps were—connections that could not be made and misperceptions requiring further work on the part of the leadership team.

Question Number 4: What's the process for exploring and modifying classroom assessment and grading practices in this district? Stakeholders will want to know how the initiative is structured, who will be making what decisions, the opportunities that will be provided for input, and the key target dates in the project time line. The school's or district's communication plan for standards-based grading must keep process (and progress) in front of the school community throughout the exploration and development process.

Question Number 3: Which stakeholders will be directly involved in the process, and how? This question and the next one may be included in the answer to Question Number 4. However it is presented, the message must be clearly communicated to the school community about which stakeholders will be involved in the exploration and development process for standards-based grading—and how they will be involved. Constituents will not and should not accept an "insiders-only" process.

Question Number 2: How will stakeholders be kept informed? The very purpose of a communication plan is to enhance and ensure effective communication. At the start of this chapter, I mentioned the importance of identifying audience, medium, and message. The communication plan should include details regarding which audiences will be targeted by which communication tools.

Question Number 1: How will this change affect me/my kid? For some parents, this is the only question in which they will be interested. The activities of Years 1 and 2 of the project transition and implementation plan (see Chapter 13) should provide steering committee members and other school or district leaders with ample information and data to answer this question as it applies to a majority of students. However, it is a bit more difficult to assure a student, or a parent of a student, who has gotten excellent grades under the present system—a known quantity—of the benefits of moving to standards-based grading—a somewhat unknown quantity. It is naïve to expect parents of high-performing students to support systemic change that promises to benefit only struggling students.

In fact, a classroom assessment and grading system that bases final grades on demonstrated academic achievement could only result in lower grades for competent students who have been able to get excellent grades through enhancements provided by points earned for work-ethic habits and extra credit. Why should those students and their parents support the change? The discussion in Chapter 2 about reassessment and preparation for college and the world of work addresses this question, but here are some additional thoughts.

Accurate grades—grades that give both students and parents a realistic view of students' preparation for success in college—will be a selling point for some. As Vatterott (2015) asks, "When do you want to find out your child doesn't know biology? Now or at the University of Iowa?" (p. 98).

Grades that are consistent across teachers of the same course or grade-level subject will appeal to a sense of fairness for many students and parents.

A system of instruction that is focused on mastery rather than coverage will appeal to those weary of the test-driven, "teach to the test and move on" instructional treadmill so prevalent in schools today. Some students and parents of students who have previously gotten easy *A*s will herald the introduction of a system of education that actually challenges capable students to demonstrate advanced achievement to earn advanced grades.

Some people may ask, "Won't our students be at a disadvantage in getting into college if it is more difficult to earn high grades at our school than it is for students in other schools with lower expectations?" The answer? Not really. College admissions officers form opinions about the academic rigor of the schools from which their students matriculate, and they know, for example, that a 3.5 grade point average from School A represents a greater likelihood of success than does a 4.0 grade point average from School B. A school that implements a comprehensive system of standards-based grading with fidelity will earn a reputation of excellence among college admissions officers.

And what about that "competent" student who has earned *A*s in the traditional system in part by being good at knowing how to "play school"? With standards-based grading, that student will have an opportunity to learn what she missed on initial assessments and demonstrate new knowledge and skills on a reassessment. So she can still earn an *A*, but under standards-based grading, that grade will reflect actual mastery of course content and skills rather than bonus points for good behavior.

That's the standards-based grading Top Ten List. A communication plan that addresses these questions and concerns will greatly enhance the chances of a project's success and sustainability.

DESTINATION 4

Competency-Based Education

• • • • • • • • • • • • • •

> After two decades of standards-based reform, a new education
> paradigm has begun to take hold—the rise of competency educa-
> tion. This new vision builds on the strong foundation of new college
> and career ready standards, challenging stakeholders to design an
> education system that emphasizes mastery of content standards
> and the transferable skills critical to success in college and today's
> workforce. (Pace, 2013, p. 3)

For most school districts, arriving at Destination 3 on the standards-
based grading continuum—Standards-Based Grading and Reporting—will
represent a huge accomplishment. A guaranteed and viable curriculum
has been created, classroom assessments are tied directly to standards-
based measurement topics and corresponding scoring scales, frequent formative assessment is embedded in instruction, and student performance
is reported by topic. Implemented with fidelity, classroom assessment and
grading is accurate, fair, and aligned with practices that encourage students'
persistence and continued learning.

However, for a few districts the vision extends beyond the confines of whole-group instruction and grade-level advancement to a personalized system of schooling in which instruction and movement through the curriculum are based on each individual student's learning progress, motivation, and goals. Standards-based measurement topics and performance standards still apply, but competency-based progression, flexible learning environments, personal learning paths, and learner profiles personalize the learning experience. Placement assessments allow students to skip units or entire courses, and grade-level distinctions become blurred or eliminated. Teachers function as diagnosticians, planners, assessors, and coaches.

KnowledgeWorks defines competency-based education as "an approach that empowers students to demonstrate mastery of a wide range of knowledge and skills at their own pace" (Pace, 2013, p. 5). The emergence of competency-based education—the last stop on our standards-based grading continuum of options—offers hope and direction for districts with a vision for truly personalizing education.

• • • • • • • • • • • • • •

The Emergence of Competency-Based Education

According to KnowledgeWorks (Pace, 2013, pp. 7–8),

- Forty states have one or more districts implementing competency-based education.

- Thirty-nine states have enacted seat-time waivers or competency-based education laws.

- The Smarter Balanced Assessment Consortium (SBAC) has launched a task force to develop recommendations for aligning SBAC assessments with emerging competency-based systems.

- Competency-based education is gaining traction in the higher education community as a growing number of colleges and universities offer competency-based options for students.

- Major philanthropic organizations have begun to invest in competency-based strategies.

A complete review and analysis of competency-based education is beyond the scope of this book. In short, with true competency-based education, everything described for Destinations 1 through 3 is in place. However, in a competency-based system, students advance standard by standard or topic by topic. Grade-level distinctions become less important, if they exist at all, and students master standards or topics rather than pass classes or subjects. Course or subject grades are eliminated, and student progress and achievement are reported by achievement levels—for example, basic, proficient, and advanced; or below grade level, at grade level, and above grade level.

Although a school or district may maintain some semblance of grouping, perhaps by grade level, for management as well as for social purposes, individuals and groups of students are able to move forward after demonstrating proficiency or better on the topic or topics at hand. Promotion and graduation are based on demonstrated mastery of the school or district's guaranteed and viable curriculum and not on seat time. Education becomes much more individualized and personalized.

The Adams 50 School District in Westminster, Colorado, moved to a K–12 competency-based system of education several years ago and has refined the program over the years to help ensure sustainability. Data from the district points to improved test score and graduation rates and a decrease in families choosing to leave the district.

The Overlap Between Competency-Based Education and Personalized Learning

A group of philanthropies and school and technology advocacy groups has put together the definition of personalized learning depicted in Figure 15.1 (Cavanagh, 2014). Competency-based education lends itself nicely to efforts to personalize education. Looking at the elements in the definition in Figure 15.1 exposes several areas of overlap.

1. **All students held to clearly defined goals and high expectations.** A school district's guaranteed and viable curriculum ensures compliance with this expectation. Standards-based measurement topics, scoring scales, and leveled assessments define learning goals and expectations for students regardless of the school or teacher to which they are assigned.

FIGURE 15.1
Personalized Learning: A Working Definition

Competency-Based Progression	Flexible Learning Environments	Personal Learning Paths	Learner Profiles
Each student's progress toward clearly defined goals is continually assessed. A student advances and earns credit as soon as he/she demonstrates mastery.	Student needs drive the design of the learning environment. All operational elements—staffing plans, space utilization, and time allocation—respond and adapt to support students in achieving their goals.	All students are held to clear, high expectations, but each student follows a customized path that responds and adapts based on his/her individual learning progress, motivations, and goals.	Each student has an up-to-date record of his/her individual strengths, needs, motivations, and goals.
Ongoing Assessment In what ways and how frequently should we assess each student's level of mastery within the dimensions that we believe are essential for his/her success?	**Operational Alignment** How might we deliver all of the learning experiences that our students need, with the resources we have available? What flexibility is in the design to enable us to respond and adapt to changing student needs?	**Personalized Learning Plans** How can we ensure that each student has a learning plan that takes into account his/her strengths, changing needs, motivations, and goals?	**Strengths & Needs** How do we capture each student's current level of mastery within each of the dimensions that we believe are essential for his/her success (e.g., academic standards, skills)? How can we highlight students' academic gaps to draw attention to their individual needs?
Individual Advancement Can individual students pursue new learning experiences as soon as they have mastered the prerequisite content? How can students attain course credit based on mastery?	**Staffing & Roles** In what ways might we structure teacher and other educator roles to support our instructional vision? What flexibility is needed to enable our staff to respond and adapt to changing student needs?	**Varied Learning Experiences (Modalities)** What types of experiences (e.g., complex tasks, experiential learning) do students need to achieve their goals? What are the ideal methods for delivering (e.g., small-group instruction, one-on-one tutoring, online learning) these experiences?	**Motivations** How might we support each student in understanding and articulating his/her interests and aspirations?

(Continues on next page)

FIGURE 15.1
Personalized Learning: A Working Definition *(continued)*

Time Allocation
In what ways might we maximize the time each student spends pursuing his/her goals? How might our student and staff schedules respond and adapt to changing student needs?

Student Ownership
In what ways might we enable students to develop and manage their own learning paths?

Information & Feedback
In what ways and how frequently might we provide timely, actionable information and feedback to students, teachers, and families?

Space Utilization
How can the design of the physical space support our instructional vision? Can we use spaces beyond our walls, and if so, how?

Goals
How might we support each student in setting personalized goals within each dimension that we believe is essential for his/her success? In what ways and how frequently might we ask students to reflect on their progress and adjust their goals accordingly?

Grouping & Connections
How should we group students to enable the varied learning experiences we hope to offer and modify to their changing needs? In what ways might we facilitate personal connections among students, and between students and adults?

Source: As first appeared in *Education Week*, October 22, 2014. Reprinted with permission from Editorial Projects in Education.

2. **Students advancing at their own pace.** Measurement topics and scoring scales can be made available to individuals or groups of students as they are ready for them, without the need to wait until the entire class has demonstrated mastery before moving on.

3. **Ongoing assessment and feedback.** All destinations on the standards-based assessment and grading continuum presented in this book emphasize the effective use of frequent formative assessment, and by definition formative assessment includes feedback to students.

4. **Student awareness of current level of performance and academic gaps.** Scoring scales provide teachers and students with a clear evaluation of what elements of a given measurement topic have been mastered, as well as the gaps in learning that need further work.

5. **Varied learning experiences.** Students in standards-based classrooms can be grouped based on where they are on the topic scoring scale. In addition to using individual and occasional whole-group instruction, a teacher can group students according to the proficiency level (2–4) they are working to attain. Membership in groups will change as individuals progress and as topics change.

6. **Student ownership.** Tracking progress based on feedback from formative assessments, recording progress by standard, and reporting achievement by measurement topic aid students in monitoring their progress and taking ownership for their learning.

• • • • • • • • • • • • • •

A standards-based assessment and grading system provides the beliefs and pedagogical infrastructure for personalizing education. Personalized, competency-based education, in turn, provides the infrastructure that enables students to succeed—in school and beyond.

Epilogue

The intent of this book is to attract and attune—to attract you to the potential of standards-based education to revolutionize teaching and learning in K–12 classrooms and to attune you to the challenges you will face and the commitment you will need to pull it off. If, having read the book, you feel a sense of great excitement and high anxiety, chances are you get it. Those two emotions tend to accompany high-impact adventures in life, and the move to standards-based education is, indeed, a high-impact adventure.

Of course, no reference book on the rationale for and processes and products of standards-based grading, no matter how well researched and thought out, is sufficient to guarantee success without competent, committed, and courageous leadership—both administrator and teacher leadership—at the school and district levels. Among the many leadership tasks involved in making a transition to standards-based grading is that of modifying the recommendations in this book to accommodate local conditions. The thoughts expressed herein represent a collection of reflections emanating from conviction and experience, not a collection of formulas subject to mathematical verification.

In the final analysis, the success or failure of standards-based education in any community must be judged by its effect on student achievement. Research on standards-based education done right strongly suggests that those who undertake it can anticipate a rich return on their investment.

Appendix A:
Two Standards-Based Units of Instruction

Algebra 1–2: Expressions, Equations, and Inequalities Unit

Learning Goal 1: Expressions		
Advanced Score 4.0	In addition to the Proficient (3.0) performance, makes in-depth inferences and extended applications of what was learned, including connections to other experiences.	The student will be able to • Create a real-life situation, write the variable expression that models it, and represent the expression in a function table.
	Proficient + Score 3.5	In addition to the complex ideas and processes (Proficient 3.0) performance, partial success at in-depth inferences and extended applications of what was learned, including connections to other experiences.
Proficient Score 3.0	No major errors or omissions regarding any of the information and simple (Basic, 2.0) or complex (Proficient, 3.0) processes that were explicitly taught.	The student will be able to • Write an expression based on data given in a function table. • Write an expression based on a real-life situation. • Create a table of values from a given expression. • Subtract expressions, correctly distributing the negative over multiple terms of the subtrahend.
	Basic + Score 2.5	No major errors or omissions regarding any of the information or simpler details and processes (Basic, 2.0) and partial knowledge of the more complex ideas and processes (Proficient, 3.0).
Basic Score 2.0	No major errors or omissions regarding the simpler details and processes (Basic, 2.0), but major errors or omissions regarding the more complex ideas and processes (Proficient, 3.0).	The student will be able to • Recognize and recall specific vocabulary. • Substitute a number for a variable and evaluate the expression. • Simplify an expression by combining like terms. • Add expressions.
Below Basic Score 1.0	A partial understanding of some of the simpler details and processes (Basic, 2.0), but major errors or omissions regarding the more complex ideas and processes.	
Failing Score 0	No evidence or insufficient evidence of student learning.	

Learning Goal 2: Equations and Inequalities		
Advanced Score 4.0	In addition to the Proficient (3.0) performance, makes in-depth inferences and extended applications of what was learned, including connections to other experiences.	The student will be able to • Write and solve a multistep equation given a real-life situation. • Describe, in writing, a real-life situation that can be solved using a given multistep equation.
	Proficient + Score 3.5	In addition to the complex ideas and processes (Proficient, 3.0) performance, partial success at in-depth inferences and extended applications of what was learned, including connections to other experiences.
Proficient Score 3.0	No major errors or omissions regarding any of the information and simple (Basic, 2.0) or complex (Proficient, 3.0) processes that were explicitly taught.	The student will be able to • Solve multistep equations. • Solve equations that contain absolute value. • Verify solutions of equations. • Apply equations to real-life situations. • Solve a literal equation for a given variable. • Write and solve a one- or two-step equation given a real-life situation.
	Basic + Score 2.5	No major errors or omissions regarding any of the information or simpler details and processes (Basic, 2.0) and partial knowledge of the more complex ideas and processes (Proficient, 3.0).
Basic Score 2.0	No major errors or omissions regarding the simpler details and processes (Basic, 2.0), but major errors or omissions regarding the more complex ideas and processes (Proficient, 3.0).	The student will be able to • Recognize and recall specific vocabulary. • Solve one and two-step equations. • Identify properties of equality. • Graph a unique solution on a number line.
Below Basic Score 1.0	A partial understanding of some of the simpler details and processes (Basic, 2.0), but major errors or omissions regarding the more complex ideas and processes (Proficient, 3.0).	
Failing Score 0	No evidence or insufficient evidence of student learning.	

Name: _____

Date: _____

Algebra 1
Expressions, Equations, and Inequalities Unit Assessment

Show your work when appropriate. Use complete sentences for all written responses. Circle your final answer.

Learning Goal 1: Expressions

Level 2/Basic

Evaluate each expression: if $x = 4$, $y = -5$, and $z = 3$

1. $\dfrac{x}{2} + 10$

2. $z - y$

Simplify each expression.

3. $5x + 7 - 9x$

4. $-3(x + 8)$

5. $3(x - 5) + 4x$

6. $(5x - 1) + (-8x + 1)$

Make a table showing the value of each expression when the value of the variable is 1, 2, 3, 4, and 5.

7. $4x - 3$

Level 3/Proficient

Simplify each expression.

8. $(2a - 3) - 4(a - 5)$

9. $(4y + 9) - (7y - 2) + (13 - y)$

Write an expression for each situation.

10. At Old Navy, jeans cost $20 a pair and fleece hoodies cost $15 each. Write a variable expression to represent the total cost of j jeans and h hoodies.

11. It costs $10 to get into an amusement park and $2 for each ride. Write a variable expression to represent the cost of riding r rides.

Level 4/Advanced

12. Create a real-life situation using complete sentences; write the variable expression that models it and represent the expression in a table of values.

Learning Goal 1 Test Score: _____

Learning Goal 2: Equations and Inequalities

Level 2/Basic

Verify whether each solution is true and show all work. Circle YES or NO.

1. $5x + 3 = 2x + 1, x = 2$

2. $-2x - 4 < 12, x = 0$

YES   NO

YES   NO

Solve each equation and circle your answer.

3. $x + 3.2 = 10.7$

4. $-45 = b - 17$

5. $-13x = -78$

6. $\dfrac{x}{6} = -12$

7. $\dfrac{4}{5}y = 16$

8. $8 - x = 15$

Solve each equation or inequality and graph the solution on the number line provided.

9. $-5p + 2 = 12$

10. $x - 10 < -13$

11. $\dfrac{x}{2} + 3 \geq 5$

Level 3/Proficient

Solve each equation.

12. $5x + 3(x + 6) = 66$

13. $4m - 16 = 2m + 4$

14. $|x + 1| = 5$

Solve each inequality.

15. $10 - 2x \geq 32$

16. $2(3x - 5) < 14$

17. $-3 < x + 5 \leq 8$

18. $3x < -12$ or $2x > 14$

Solve each equation for the indicated variable.

19. $I = Prt$ (Solve for P)   20. $r = s - t$ (Solve for s)

Write an equation or inequality and solve, if necessary.

21. The bowling alley charges $2 to rent shoes and $3.50 per game. If Micah spent a total of $12.50, how many games did he bowl?

22. At Worlds of Fun, you must be at least 48 inches tall to ride the roller coasters. Write the inequality that represents how tall a person must be in order to meet the height requirement. Use h to represent height.

Level 4/Advanced

Choose 2 of 3.

23. Hannah wants to hire a painter to paint her house. Painters Plus charges a fee of $360 plus $12 per hour. Davis and Sons charges a fee of $279 plus $15 per hour. Write and solve an equation to determine the number of hours for which the two costs would be the same. Show all work. Write your final answer in a complete sentence.

24. Create your own real-life situation that could be modeled by the following equation: $2x + 25 = 75$. Solve the equation.

25. Write a real-life situation that could be modeled by the following inequality: $5x \leq 100$. Solve the inequality.

Learning Goal 2 Test Score: _____

Child Development 1–2 Proficiency Scale

Topic: Birth Defects

Level of Performance	Score	Description
Advanced	4	In addition to 3.0 performance, in-depth inferences and applications that go beyond what was taught. The student will be able to • Examine the ethical, legal, social, and personal implications of genetic testing for birth defects. • Determine the benefits and drawbacks of genetic counseling. • Develop a bill to protect the rights of children from environmental birth defects.
Proficient	3.5	In addition to 3.0 performance, partial success at inferences and applications that go beyond what was taught.

(Continues on next page)

Proficient	3	No major errors or omissions regarding any of the information or processes (simple or complex) that were explicitly taught. The student will be able to • Compare and contrast environmental and genetic birth defects. • Compare the impact of the stage of prenatal development with the types of environmental birth defect exposures. • Determine ways to help lessen the impact of birth defects before and after birth. • Analyze possible consequences that families or individuals may face when determining whether to undergo genetic counseling or testing.
Basic	2.5	No major errors or omissions regarding the simpler details or processes and partial knowledge of the more complex ideas and processes.
Basic	2	No major errors or omissions regarding the simpler details or processes but major errors or omissions regarding the more complex ideas and processes. The student will be able to • Recognize or recall specific vocabulary such as *birth defect, genetic birth defect,* and *environmental birth defect.* • Determine ways to help prevent birth defects. • Explain the types of testing used to determine birth defects. • Name common birth defects and what may have caused them. These could include *club foot, cleft palate, Phenylketonuria (PKU), cerebral palsy, color blindness, fetal alcohol syndrome, cystic fibrosis (CF), Down syndrome, Fragile X syndrome, sickle cell disease,* and so on.
Below Basic	1.5	Partial knowledge of the simpler details or processes, but major errors or omissions regarding the more complex ideas and processes.
Below Basic	1.0	With help, a partial understanding of some of the simpler details and processes and some of the more complex ideas and processes.
Failing	0	No evidence or demonstration of student learning.

Birth Defects Formative Assessment

Basic Items (Level 2):

Match each of the following birth defects with its correct definition.

_____ 1. Down syndrome

_____ 2. PKU

_____ 3. Cerebral palsy

_____ 4. Club foot

_____ 5. Cleft palate

_____ 6. Spinal bifida

a. Way in which the body processes proteins that, if not addressed through diet, causes mental retardation.

b. Malformed tissue creates an opening between the roof of the mouth and the nasal cavity.

c. Spinal column does not completely close around the spinal cord.

d. Foot and ankle bones, joints, muscles, and blood vessels are formed incorrectly.

e. An extra chromosome is present at birth.

f. Muscles are difficult to control.

Proficient Items (Level 3):

7. Provide the pros and cons for genetic counseling and testing during pregnancy.

	Pros	Cons
Genetic counseling before pregnancy.		
Implications for the family if genetic testing determines a birth defect.		
A family is considering a pregnancy. There have been some birth defects among family members. Explain your recommendation on genetic counseling and testing based on your research and thinking.		

8. List 3 environmental birth defects and how they could be avoided by good prenatal decisions and health.

Environmental birth defect	Recommended prenatal care and health decisions

Advanced (Level 4):

9. You are part of a legislative committee drafting a bill that will help with the prevention of birth defects. Write your bill considering the following:
   a. Which birth defect you will target for prevention.
   b. Which behaviors of the mother during pregnancy you will encourage to change.
   c. How you will convince the mother and society to change these behaviors.
   d. Information or research that will help you to achieve your goal.
   e. Arguments from opposing groups that may defeat your proposed legislation.

Source: Copyright 2016 by Karen Spencer-May. Used with permission.

Appendix B:
Schools and Districts Implementing Some Form of Standards-Based Grading

Anchorage School District, Alaska (http://www.asdk12.org/)

Ankeny Community School District, Iowa (http://www.ankenyschools.org/)

Bellevue Public Schools, Nebraska (http://www.bellevuepublicschools.org/)

Bloomington Public Schools, Minnesota (https://www.bloomington.k12.mn.us/)

Catalina Foothills School District, Arizona (http://www.cfsd16.org/public/home.aspx)

Collier County Public Schools, Florida (http://www.collierschools.com/)

Cumberland High School, Rhode Island (http://www.cumberlandschools.org/content/cumberland-high-school)

Des Moines Public Schools, Iowa (http://www.dmschools.org/)

East Union Middle/High School, Iowa (http://eastunion.ia.euc.schoolinsites.com/)

Farmington Municipal Schools, New Mexico (http://district.fms.k12.nm.us/)

Grafton School District, Wisconsin (http://www.grafton.k12.wi.us/)

Grand Island Public Schools, Nebraska (http://www.gips.org/)

Greenwood Middle/High School, Wisconsin (http://www.greenwood.k12.wi.us/middlehigh/index.cfm)

James Campbell High School, Hawaii (http://www.campbellhigh.org/)

Kettle Moraine School District, Wisconsin (http://www.kmsd.edu/)

Lindsay Unified School District, California (http://www.lindsay.k12.ca.us/)

Madison Metropolitan School District, Wisconsin (https://www.madison.k12.wi.us/)

Milwaukee Public Schools, Wisconsin (http://mps.milwaukee.k12.wi.us/)

Minneapolis Public Schools, Minnesota (http://www.mpls.k12.mn.us/)

Minnetonka High School, Minnesota (http://www.minnetonka.k12.mn.us/MHS)

North Thurston Public Schools, Washington (http://www.nthurston.k12.wa.us/)

Oak Creek Franklin Joint School District, Wisconsin (http://www.ocfsd.org/)

Osseo Area Schools, Minnesota (http://www.district279.org/)

Papillion La Vista Community Schools, Nebraska (http://www.plcschools.org/)

Park Hill School District, Missouri (https://www.parkhill.k12.mo.us/)

Sanborn Regional High School, New Hampshire (http://web.sau17.org/index.php/schools-188/high-school)

School District 67, BC, Canada (http://www.sd67.bc.ca/)

Solon Community School District, Iowa (http://www.solon.k12.ia.us/)

Spring Lake Park Schools, Minnesota (http://www.springlakeparkschools.org/)

Van Meter Community School District, Iowa (http://www.vmbulldogs.com/)

Wauwatosa School district, Wisconsin (http://www.wauwatosa.k12.wi.us/)

West Ada School District, Idaho (http://www.westada.org/domain/3649)

Westside Community Schools, Nebraska (http://www.westside66.org/)

West York Area School District, Pennsylvania (http://www.wyasd.k12.pa.us/)

References

Barber, M., & Mourshed, M. (2007). *How the world's best-performing school systems come out on top*. London: McKinsey.

Cavanagh, S. (2014, October 20). What is "personalized learning"? Educators seek clarity. *Education Week, 34*(09), s2, s4. Available: http://www.edweek.org/ew/articles/2014/10/22/09pl-overview.h34.html

Chappuis, J. (2014, March). Thoughtful assessment with the learner in mind. *Educational Leadership, 71*(6), 20–26.

Danielson, C. (2007). *Enhancing professional practice: A framework for teaching*. Alexandria, VA: ASCD.

Dressel, P. (1957). Facts and fancy in assigning grades. *Basic College Quarterly, 2*. East Lansing, MI: Michigan State University.

Duke Today (2006). Duke study: Homework helps students succeed in school, as long as there isn't too much. Available: http://today.duke.edu/2006/03/homework.html

Earl, L. M. (2003). *Assessment as learning: Using classroom assessment to maximize student learning*. Thousand Oaks, CA: Corwin.

Fernández-Alonso, R., Suárez-Álvarez, J., & Muñiz, J. (2015, March 16). Adolescents' homework performance in mathematics and science: Personal factors and teaching practices. *Journal of Educational Psychology, 107*(4), 1075–1083. doi.org/10.1037/edu0000032

Fisher, D., & Frey, N. (2008). *Better learning through structured teaching*. Alexandria, VA: ASCD.

Fullan, M. (2006). *Turnaround leadership*. San Francisco: Jossey-Bass.

Guskey, T. (2004). Zero alternatives. *Principal Leadership, 5*(2), 49–53.

Guskey, T. (2009). *Practical solutions for serious problems in standards-based grading*. Thousand Oaks, CA: Corwin.

Guskey, T. (2013, September). The case against percentage grades. *Educational Leadership, 71*(1), 68–72.

Heflebower, T., Hoegh, J. K., & Warrick, P. (2014). *A school leader's guide to standards-based grading*. Bloomington, IN: Marzano Research Laboratory.

Madgic, R. F. (1988). The point system of grading: A critical appraisal. *NASSP Bulletin, 72*(507), 29–34.

March, J. K., & Peters, K. H. (2015). Telling the truth about the Common Core. *Phi Delta Kappan, 96*(8), 63–65.

Marzano, R. J. (2006). *Classroom assessment & grading that work.* Alexandria, VA: ASCD.

Marzano, R. J. (2007). *The art and science of teaching: A comprehensive framework for effective instruction.* Alexandria, VA: ASCD.

Marzano, R. J., Warrick, P., & Simms, J. A. (2014). *A handbook for high reliability schools: The next steps in school reform.* Bloomington, IN: Marzano Research Laboratory.

Marzano, R. J., & Haystead, M. W. (2008). *Making standards useful in the classroom.* Alexandria, VA: ASCD.

National Governors Association Center for Best Practices & Council of Chief State School Officers. (2010). *Common Core State Standards.* Washington, DC: Author.

O'Connor, K. (2009a). *How to grade for learning, K–12.* Thousand Oaks, CA: Corwin.

O'Connor, K. (2009b). Reforming grading practices in secondary schools. *Principal's Research Review 4*(1), 1–7.

O'Connor, K. (2010). *A repair kit for grading: 15 fixes for broken grades.* Upper Saddle River, NJ: Pearson.

Pace, L. (2013). *An emerging federal role for competency education.* Competency Education Series: Policy Brief One. Cincinnati, OH: KnowledgeWorks. Available: http://www.knowledgeworks.org/sites/default/files/Competency-Education-Series%20-Policy-Brief-One.pdf

Popham, W. J. (2008). *Transformative assessment.* Alexandria, VA: ASCD.

Reeves, D. B. (2004). The case against the zero. *Phi Delta Kappan, 86*(4), 324–325.

Reeves, D. B. (2008a, February). Leading to change: Effective grading practices. *Educational Leadership, 65*(5), 85–87.

Reeves, D. B. (2008b). *Reframing teacher leadership to improve your school.* Alexandria, VA: ASCD.

Suskind, D. (2012). What students would do if they did not do their homework. *Phi Delta Kappan, 94*(1), 52–55.

Vatterott, C. (2015). *Rethinking grading: Meaningful assessment for standards-based learning.* Alexandria, VA: ASCD.

Wormeli, R. (2006). *Fair isn't equal: Assessing and grading in differentiated classrooms.* Portland, ME: Stenhouse Publishers & the National Middle School Association.

Wormeli, R. (2011). Redos and retakes done right. *Educational Leadership, 69*(3), 22–26.

Yoon, K. S., Duncan, T., Lee, S. W., Scarloss, B., & Shapley, K. L. (2007). *Reviewing the evidence on how teacher professional development affects student achievement* (Issues & Answers Report, REL 2007-No. 033). Washington, DC: U.S. Department of Education, Institute of Education Sciences, National Center for Education Evaluation and Regional Assistance, Regional Educational Laboratory Southwest. Retrieved from http://ies.ed.gov/ncee/edlabs

Index

Page references followed by an italicized *f* indicate information contained in figures.

About the Author

Tim R. Westerberg served as a school principal for 26 years, the last 20 of which were at Littleton High School in Colorado. Prior to entering school administration, he taught social studies and coached in Illinois and Iowa. He currently lives in Dillon, Colorado, and works nationally and internationally as a school improvement coach.

Dr. Westerberg served on the NASSP/Carnegie Foundation Commission on the Restructuring of the American High School, which produced the seminal report *Breaking Ranks: Changing an American Institution,* and he played a significant role in the development of *Breaking Ranks II,* which was released in 2004. Other professional activities include serving as a member of ASCD's The Art and Science of Teaching professional development faculty, president of the Colorado Association of School Executives, member of the Colorado Commission for High School Improvement, and executive director of the Alliance for Quality Teaching.

Dr. Westerberg was named one of four finalists for the NASSP/Met Life Principal of the Year program in 1994 and received the Honor Administrator Award by the Colorado Music Educators Association in 1998 and the Department Service Award by the Colorado Association of Secondary School Principals in 1999. He is the author of numerous articles and two books in addition to this one: *Creating the High Schools of Our Choice* (Eye on Education, 2007) and *Becoming a Great High School: 6 Strategies and 1 Attitude That Make a Difference* (ASCD, 2009).

Related ASCD Resources

At the time of publication, the following ASCD resources were available (ASCD stock numbers in parentheses). For up-to-date information about ASCD resources, go to www.ascd.org. This book relates to the **challenged** tenet of ASCD's Whole Child Initiative; to learn more about this initiative, go to www.ascd.org/wholechild. Search the complete archives of *Educational Leadership* at www.ascd.org/el.

ASCD EDge®

Exchange ideas and connect with other educators on the social networking site ASCD EDge at http://ascdedge.ascd.org.

Print Products

Classroom Assessment and Grading That Work by Robert J. Marzano (#106006)

Grading and Group Work: How Do I Assess Individual Learning When Students Work Together? (ASCD Arias) by Susan M. Brookhart (#SF113073)

Grading Smarter, Not Harder: Assessment Strategies That Motivate Kids and Help Them Learn by Myron Dueck (#114003)

How to Create and Use Rubrics for Formative Assessment and Grading by Susan M. Brookhart (#112001)

Making Standards Useful in the Classroom by Robert J. Marzano and Mark W. Haystead (#108006)

Rethinking Grading: Meaningful Assessment for Standards-Based Learning by Cathy Vatterott (#115001)

DVD

Smarter Assessment in the Secondary Classroom DVD by Myron Dueck (#616045)

ASCD PD Online® Course

Using Data to Determine Student Mastery (#PD14OC001M)

For more information: send e-mail to member@ascd.org; call 1-800-933-2723 or 703-578-9600, press 2; send a fax to 703-575-5400; or write to Information Services, ASCD, 1703 N. Beauregard St., Alexandria, VA 22311-1714 USA.